# Memoirs of an Unfinished Tale

# Memoirs of an Unfinished Tale

## A Performance of Acts of the Apostles

*With Application Questions*
*for Study and Discussion*

## Mark F. Whitters

CASCADE *Books* · Eugene, Oregon

MEMOIRS OF AN UNFINISHED TALE
A Performance of Acts of the Apostles

Cascade Books
An Imprint of Wipf and Stock Publishers
199 W. 8th Ave., Suite 3
Eugene, OR 97401

www.wipfandstock.com

PAPERBACK ISBN: 978-1-5326-1126-1
HARDCOVER ISBN: 978-1-5326-1128-5
EBOOK ISBN: 978-1-5326-1127-8

*Cataloguing-in-Publication data:*

Names: Whitters, Mark F., author.

Title: Memoirs of an unfinished tale : a performance of Acts of the Apostles / Mark F. Whitters.

Description: Eugene, OR: Cascade Books, 2017 | Includes index.

Identifiers: ISBN 978-1-5326-1126-1 (paperback) | ISBN 978-1-5326-1128-5 (hardcover) | ISBN 978-1-5326-1127-8 (ebook)

Subjects: LCSH: Bible. Acts—Criticism, interpretation, etc.

Classification: BS2625.52 W55 2017 (print) | BS2625.52 (ebook).

Manufactured in the U.S.A.                              JUNE 7, 2017

# Contents

# Contents

# CONTENTS

# Contents

# Figures and Illustrations

# Preface

What if Luke had to reteach the basic lessons of his history of the early Church? What stories contained the nuggets he would impart to the neophyte recipient he called Theophilus? How would he communicate his point while livening up the details for someone who either was not present for the actual event or had not paid sufficient attention the first time he wrote Acts of the Apostles?

This is Luke's retelling his second book to a younger and still eager Theophilus. According to the sequence, the two books are bridged by the life of Jesus—and this current work focuses on what happens *after* Jesus. It presumes Theophilus knows the details of the Gospel of Luke. Luke realizes that if he is to arouse his reader to act on what he remembers about Jesus, he must again reenact his stories and replay the events before Theophilus's very eyes. He knows that Theophilus is interested in history not as a dry memorization of facts nor of a metal chain of events, but as a compendium of lessons that guide growth and change. History, thinks Luke, unfolds as episodes, cohering around an intelligible theme with drama and suspense. So, not unlike a play, it requires imaginative performance to both entertain and provoke an audience to react.

What follows therefore is Luke's representation of Acts of the Apostles, but it appears improvisionally here as an emerging and entertaining drama. It springs to life from its original literary roots. Think of what follows as a play performed by one actor who stands with one foot on stage and one foot in real life, a creative project with episodes guided by the original text. This cycle of viewing and reviewing past events to derive current meaning constitutes what the ancient Greeks believed about the study of history— and it is a good principle to facilitate the reading of the Bible for anyone.

The performance below reformulates in modern language what Luke might say to an audience today. At the same time it selects and highlights particular episodes and details instead of repeating the whole story. While it may not cover each verse and reference that a full commentary does, it hopefully will narrate the line of adventures that ties the book together and then can shed light on everything that a more thorough reading of Acts of the Apostles brings out.

The presentation corresponds closely to the layout of Acts of the Apostles, that is, it follows the chapter-by-chapter development of the book. It divides each chapter into episodes that the reader can follow in regular intervals, day by day and week by week. Alternatively, the episodes often stand independently enough that one can consult them for particular interpretations. One particular application of this representation is that it allows for a dramatic *performance* of Acts as a method of reaching an audience. This method of teaching is particularly useful in today's "virtual reality" world.

Finally, at the end of each episode within this representation of Acts of the Apostles are questions geared for an individual reader or (with slight modifications) an audience. The questions are based on the lessons of the episodes as laid out, but are updated for modern and sometimes secular contexts.

**Fig. 1: *The Narrator*, by Jamie Treadwell.
Used with the permission of the artist.**

# Acknowledgments

Any writer knows that the creative enterprise involves many sources of inspiration. In my case I credit two dedicated readers, Larry Lahey and Joseph Matthias. Professor Lahey endured the malapropisms of my prose, while Joseph, poet extraordinaire and director of University Christian Outreach at the University of Michigan, the doggerels of my poetry.

I had the good fortune of enlisting the aesthetic talents of two noted artists, Jamie Treadwell (confrere) and Yvette Rock (co-worker in Detroit), whose illustrations reimagine what Acts of the Apostles narrates. The impetus to write comes from my association with a new pedagogical method in the liberal arts called Reacting—and here I credit Mark Carnes of Barnard College for developing and promoting this style of education, as well as his disciple and my colleague in History & Philosophy at Eastern Michigan University, Mark Higbee.

Finally, I am truly inspired by my longsuffering confreres, Dave O'Connor and Ed Conlin, who untiringly dream new things for bringing unity and healing to Detroit and tolerate with humor every idiosyncrasy I manifest and innovation I concoct. "*Sanctis qui sunt in terra eius mirificavit mihi omnes voluntates meas in eis*" (Ps 16 [15]:3). As for the saints in the land, he has made them wonderful. I know.

# Introduction

## Greetings, Theophilus!

Theophilus, forgive my playfulness, but I want to perform for you live what I once had reported in my history of events after the life of Jesus. This time, though, I will sing a new tune, dance a different step, dress up some dingy details, strum out a soliloquy so as to amuse and inform you.

I want you to relive this history with me. Earlier I set it before you as an elder to a younger, a teacher to a pupil, maybe even a father to a son; but I sensed that I failed to entice you to continued study and life-long learning. Yes, I admit my history was a bit dense for a deeper immersion in spiritual waters, so I hope this second try arouses your imaginative energies to recreate a life of wonder and joy about what lies ahead for us.

As you know, Theophilus, I never dashed off a formal ending to my book. And why not? Because I wanted you to envision how it would end if you were in the story—and so write a conclusion suited to its aims. You are, after all, the target audience for my whole project of writing things down. I wanted to make sure that you would know how the Kingdom of God really appeared in our day, beginning from the appearance of the one called John the Baptist until the arrival of Paul in Rome.

## Second Half

I finished the first half of the project about Jesus up to the time of his resurrection from the dead. One of these days, we will sit down and go over these details once again. It is the second half that takes into account you—and all of us—and that part is unfinished. Now I will retell Acts, sticking with the story but enlivening it with fresh routines. In a way, I am retelling it

1

as much for myself as for you. So I invite you to come along as I relive my memories.

It doesn't really matter where you were in those exciting early days, whether you were connected with John the Baptist's movement or whether you saw Jesus with your own eyes either while he was first alive or afterwards. It was like a play that we were living out, a dance already choreographed. The script was already jotted down and the steps already rehearsed, and now its story and action envelope both of us.

Will you join in the performance, Theophilus, and complete its drama—even if you were not in the original cast? Will you let my writing coax your participation? So let me now go over the second half of the story again, at least what I think are the key points, since it is still fresh in your mind and speaks to what you will do with your life.

The question I am raising in my book is, Will you continue what has begun?

# Chapter 1

## The Commission

When we had Jesus with us over those forty days after he had risen from the dead, we all thought that he would bring things to a close straightaway, that the agenda for the Kingdom we had always dreamed about was now fulfilled. The Kingdom! It brought to our minds visions of David and Solomon and vindication for the oppressed and for the poor. If such had been the case, I probably would not have written anything and just waited until the end of the forty days. Instead, Jesus told us something that took us by surprise: there would be more "times and seasons." He made the Kingdom sound like a cooperative venture involving him working through us. The times and seasons are in divine hands, but the continuation of what he began was in our hands.

He told us that God would invest us with his presence spiritually, and we would see an expansion of the Kingdom into surrounding lands, not just Jewish domains but worldwide. He implied that this would take time and would involve people like you and me, Theophilus. We would receive in time the power to expand what Jesus had begun and was continuing through us: our role was primarily to be available and to witness what would happen.

Then all of a sudden he began to ascend as if carried up by clouds and disappearing into them at the same time. Right before our eyes, just after he told us that the Kingdom depended on us, it seemed that he was demonstrating what he meant. You see, Theophilus, he was saying that he was as close as the mist and clouds to our daily life, just not *completely* visible to us. Occasionally we see the Kingdom in the form of the brilliant sun, but most often its glory is shrouded until the day when Jesus returns through

3

the clouds and exposes the Kingdom's fullness. Let me repeat a bit of what I wrote you about it back then and give you some questions to think about.

> Acts 1:4–9 [4] And while staying with them he charged them not to depart from Jerusalem, but to wait for the promise of the Father, which, he said, "you heard from me, [5] for John baptized with water, but before many days you shall be baptized with the Holy Spirit." [6] So when they had come together, they asked him, "Lord, will you at this time restore the kingdom to Israel?" [7] He said to them, "It is not for you to know times or seasons which the Father has fixed by his own authority. [8] But you shall receive power when the Holy Spirit has come upon you; and you shall be my witnesses in Jerusalem and in all Judea and Samaria and to the end of the earth." [9] And when he had said this, as they were looking on, he was lifted up, and a cloud took him out of their sight.

1.  Are there "times and seasons" of history that point to the ebb and flow of grace and divine visitations? Do these times and seasons show the sovereignty of God?

2.  What are the times and seasons in my life that point to my own growth and maturity? Reflect on the major events in the last year. How would I classify these events as times and seasons?

3.  When can I point to the presence of Jesus as if hovering over me in a cloud? How do I recognize the glory of God in the midst of daily life? Can I sometimes see the glory of God shining through the clouds?

## Contemplation, Waiting, Action

We stood there amazed and transfixed, as if somehow we could pierce the mist into which he faded. Our loss of his immediate presence was tangible—we were the ones who knew him from the start and thought he would do it all for us and not through us.

Then we sensed the presence of divine messengers who goaded us down from this place, this mountain of contemplation. How long would we stay merely "men of Galilee," unsophisticated and garish in our ways? How long would we be fishermen and farmers and workers who knew Jesus, and followed him—but only to the degree of our comfort zone? We were standing there on that mountain, as if frozen in place.

But this was not Jesus's last commission to us. We men of Galilee were to go back down to Jerusalem to face the same opposition Jesus had faced, and we were to remain there and wait. Otherwise the mountain stood only for pregnant possibility and fertile imagination. The implication was that once we faced the world of Jerusalem, then Judea, Samaria, and the end of the earth were for the taking. He had ordered us back to our tenuous positions, and it was sanctioned by these divine messengers. Somehow our rustic Galilean ways were to be gilded for action, and we could not stay on the mountain any longer gazing at what we once observed while Jesus was with us and what we hoped might be.

I tell you this, Theophilus, because I am summoning you to take action yourself. I am reassuring you that the mountain of the cloud is not far off when you need to contemplate—only a Sabbath's day away. There will be days when apparent losses need to reckoned and accepted. These are days of contemplation. Yet most of our lives are spent in the meantime, the other six days of the week, and this involves action and sometimes abject toil.

Still, keep in mind, Theophilus, the angels also reassure us that there will be another divine incursion one day. The fact that this mountain, a "Sabbath-day's journey from Jerusalem," is the place of contemplation shows that prayer is never too far away from action. Prayer allows us to climb a mountain as a place of divine appointment and consecration, but we must resolutely return at the right time.

> Acts 1:10–12 [10] And while they were gazing into heaven as he went, behold, two men stood by them in white robes, [11] and said, "Men of Galilee, why do you stand looking into heaven? This Jesus, who was taken up from you into heaven, will come in the same way as you saw him go into heaven." [12] Then they returned to Jerusalem from the mount called Olivet, which is near Jerusalem, a sabbath day's journey away . . .

1. Can I identify some "mountain-top" experiences I have had? How long do they linger in the "times and seasons" that follow?

2. Do I feel I have the right balance of contemplating Jesus in the circumstances around me and taking action on his behalf? How can I occasionally get away, "a Sabbath day's journey away" from my circumstances?

3. Do I feel qualified to do the mission that Jesus has given me? Why or why not? What things make me feel unqualified as mere "men of Galilee" for the work I must do in Jerusalem and elsewhere?

# Dice

That first generation of leaders and followers was an awesome group. They were chosen, and you might even say destined to take on the responsibility of continuing what Jesus had begun. I say destined because the whole program and structure of what we call the Church, the assembly of those called by God, conformed to a design and a plan. We did not establish this design or plan, and in fact we left it pretty much as Jesus had set it up.

First, "the Twelve." They are the ones who spent time with Jesus, and whom Jesus designated as stand-ins for the twelve tribes of Israel. You may remember that God first called Abraham, who was promised land and off-spring as great as could be imagined. This promise was entrusted to Abraham and his twelve grandsons, themselves stand-ins for the twelve tribes now called Israel. So these were the Twelve we looked to fulfill the design and plan of God. You may remember that we called them "Apostles"—a word which means "delegates" or "messengers." So we can suppose them to be delegates for all Israel.

Since Judas had betrayed Jesus and in despair at his act killed himself, we all knew that another one of us—one who spent time with Jesus and who would stand publicly to declare that Jesus rose from the dead—needed to replace the traitor.

We needed to fill out the number of the Twelve. While Judas stood for a tribe with its own encampment (ἔπαυλις, *epaulis*, means "frontier station") and his inheritance among the Twelve was lost now, his job or position as "inspector" (ἐπισκοπή, *episkopē*) needed replacement. We would entrust this office to someone with personal knowledge through first-hand contact with Jesus.

We were so convinced that this whole thing was providentially arranged that we rejected human voting or selection methods for finding a replacement for Judas. Jesus was so present to us, though still hidden in the clouds, that we just cast lots for the right person. As you may recognize, Greeks regard fate and destiny and the powers of "luck" to be greater and more fearsome than the gods. Not so for us! Even these forces are in the hands of God, and so we can trust these outcomes to be a part of divine providence and care. We have a proverb that reads, "The lot is cast into the lap, but the decision is wholly from the Lord."[1] Random chances are not outside of divine control.

See what I mean about this first generation being destined to fulfill God's design and plan? As long as we did our part, the rest was in God's hands. You can begin to see the reverence we held for this institution led by Twelve—and along with the Scriptures themselves, it is clear that we should regard its origin and authority as divinely ordained. Theophilus, you will find in all my writings a sense of fulfillment either of Church expansion or of the intent of the Scriptures. How little depends on votes, tests, or connections. Providence is a divine prerogative, and there is no reason to fear it!

Acts 1:16–26 **16** "Brethren, the scripture had to be fulfilled, which the Holy Spirit spoke beforehand by the mouth of David, concerning Judas who was guide to those who arrested Jesus. **17** For he was numbered among us, and was allotted his share in this ministry. **18** (Now this man bought a field with the reward of his wickedness; and falling headlong he burst open in the middle and all his bowels gushed out. **19** And it became known to all the inhabitants of Jerusalem, so that the field was called in their language Akeldama, that is, Field of Blood.) **20** For it is written in the book of Psalms, 'Let his habitation become desolate, and let there be no one to live in it'; and 'His office let another take.' **21** So one of the men who have accompanied us during all the time that the Lord Jesus went in and out among us, **22** beginning from the baptism of John until the day when he was taken up from us—one of these men must become with us a witness to his resurrection." **23** And they put forward two, Joseph called Barsabbas, who was surnamed Justus, and Matthias. **24** And they prayed and said, "Lord, who knowest the hearts of all men, show which one of these two thou hast chosen **25** to take the place in this ministry and apostleship from which Judas turned aside, to go to his own place." **26** And they cast lots for them, and the lot fell on Matthias; and he was enrolled with the eleven apostles.

1. How would I describe an apostle in my own words? What are the words used in the text to describe the apostleship of Judas? Is the ministry of an apostle something I can relate to and respect? Why

---

1. Prov 16:33.

or why not? How would I describe the text's attitude toward the first generation of apostles?

2. How do I believe that the Church is divinely appointed and destined? How do I regard its rulings and judgments?

3. What is my attitude about the direction that "luck" is taking me? Would I consider it providential or just blind? Do I try to fight a sense that life is out of my hands?

# Chapter 2

## Seasons

As I mentioned above, we are participants in a story already told. You get a sense for that in the way that the main characters—people like Peter and Paul and James—cite the precedents for their deeds in the writings of the Scriptures. I am recording a history for which events have already been ordained. Consider it: Jesus speaks with us for forty days, then sends us back into the city where he had envisioned his mission being accomplished. There we pray for ten more days until the time of Pentecost. During these ten days, we reconstitute the measure and office of the Twelve which Jesus had summoned to conform to the tribes of Israel, and we are so certain that God will fulfill this blueprint that we leave it up to a roll of the dice to determine. Who is in control? Who calls the shots?

Now let me speak about this preordained event, Pentecost. As you may have learned, it is a feast of harvest time—but not the first and not the final fruits. In God's timing, there is something that conforms to the symbolism of calendar: it is not by chance that our summons to mobilize happened during this season.

We were told to stay put and wait until we were invested by God with some kind of power. No one expected a bunch of Galileans, rustics and uncouth Jews all of us, to amount to much. But something drew us altogether daily for prayer and reminiscing for ten days, climaxing on the very day of Pentecost.

During that morning we all had an experience that shook each of us: it seemed like a rush of wind and was followed by a burning of fire. We began uttering in ecstasy what sounded like languages, which I can only describe as spiritual communications. We felt that we needed to let go what was bottled up within us, and the result was transmissions from the spirit world.

We took to the streets where there were pilgrims who had come to Jerusalem for the feast. They were like an audience ready-made for our stage: people from all over the world who were already in place to hear us babble about the Kingdom in words that they also instinctively understood no matter their background. You've heard of Babel, Theophilus, where an earthly kingdom tried to build a tower and ended up dividing by language? Well, this was like the tower of Babel in reverse. Instead of words dividing humanity, now words were uniting those who identified with a heavenly Kingdom.

With all of these ethnic groups before us, was this the beginning of what Jesus had said about being witnesses to the ends of the earth? Was Pentecost the symbol that the next harvest was ready? I tell you, Theophilus, in retrospect the whole thing unfolded like it was according to script.

At first, this experience caused some bewilderment and misunderstanding. "Who are these Galilean yahoos to talk about the finer points of theology? What do they know?" Yet we knew something had taken hold of us, and we stood our ground in the face of savants and scholars from all over the world. And these were people whom you think would jump on the bandwagon of the Kingdom—they were already committed enough to travel from afar to observe Pentecost in Jerusalem. But they were zealous by half again too much. We will notice this same attitude when we size up Paul later in my narrative.

You know what I am saying, Theophilus? It takes a while for something new to be accepted even by supporters and friends. Now remember this, Theophilus: when the Kingdom appears, even the religious "Status Quo" is never fully on-board. Sometimes what you will witness is that God has to clear the deck before the boat is ready to sail. That is what we found out in the streets of Jerusalem that Pentecost day.

Consider my words, and these following questions, before I continue my review.

1.  How does God seem to act in consonance with the seasons of life? Can I remember any spiritual experience that conformed to what was going on in the "real world?"

2.  Have I—like the Galilean followers of Jesus—ever felt totally unqualified and yet compelled to share an insight with a group? Did I share it?

3. Have I ever felt inspired to share something with a group and found that it fell flat on its face? Or when my experience met with divided opinions about its validity, what was my response?

4. Have I ever been a part of something new and exciting—filled with the Spirit, so to speak—and been criticized or ridiculed for it?

5. Look carefully at my own attitude toward simple believers: do I ever make fun of simple and trusting faith as being naïve or foolish?

6. Can I think of various ways that the works of the Spirit are derided (though not specifically and frontally persecuted) in the modern world?

> Acts 2:1–13 [1]When the day of Pentecost had come, they were all together in one place. [2] And suddenly a sound came from heaven like the rush of a mighty wind, and it filled all the house where they were sitting. [3] And there appeared to them tongues as of fire, distributed and resting on each one of them. [4] And they were all filled with the Holy Spirit and began to speak in other tongues, as the Spirit gave them utterance. [5] Now there were dwelling in Jerusalem Jews, devout men from every nation under heaven. [6] And at this sound the multitude came together, and they were bewildered, because each one heard them speaking in his own language. [7] And they were amazed and wondered, saying, "Are not all these who are speaking Galileans? [8] And how is it that we hear, each of us in his own native language? [9] Parthians and Medes and Elamites and residents of Mesopotamia, Judea and Cappadocia, Pontus and Asia, [10] Phrygia and Pamphylia, Egypt and the parts of Libya belonging to Cyrene, and visitors from Rome, both Jews and proselytes, [11] Cretans and Arabians, we hear them telling in our own tongues the mighty works of God." [12] And all were amazed and perplexed, saying to one another, "What does this mean?" [13] But others mocking said, "They are filled with new wine."

## Outpouring

Something had taken hold of Peter as an individual after that wind and fire moment in the upper room. Almost in spite of himself, Peter gave a speech punctuated by Scriptures that seemed to come out of nowhere as he stood before the large crowd.

I won't relate the whole speech now—go back and read it for yourself. But I will tell you two things now that dawned on me like the rising sun. First, he said three times that Pentecost was about an "outpouring." The wind, the fire, the tongues all were indiscriminate and inundating. When a dam breaks, the water goes everywhere and sweeps across everything. Nobody is left untouched and nothing stays the same. The power is seemingly oblivious to the recipients.

Second, Peter quoted from the prophet Joel about men and women, young and old both collaborating in prophecy, visions, and dreams to prepare for the Kingdom. The power is oblivious to one's sex and age. The young need to see something to contribute to the future, and so they will see visions for themselves and the mission. The elders, on the other hand, dream. They reflect on the past and now use their fund of knowledge to speculate on what is possible given the circumstances. Courage of the young with judgment of the old. Both work in harmony in "the last days" before the Kingdom arrives. What is striking, Theophilus, is that the Kingdom will unfold through cross-generational bonds—and each stage of life does what is suitable for its age.

1. What kind of future can I imagine, based on the Holy Spirit being poured on me?

2. How should I reflect on my past activities in order to impart depth to ongoing things?

**Fig. 2:** *I Will Pour Out My Spirit*, **by Yvette Rock.**
**Used with the permission of the artist.**

## Peter as Witness

Towards the end of Peter's speech, he uttered a word that made us remember what Jesus had said to us while we contemplated his departure on the Mount of Olives: "witnesses." He had said, "You will be my witnesses . . . to the ends of the earth." And Peter now said the same thing: "We are all witnesses." Theophilus, this is the key to our cooperation with him in expanding the Kingdom. What is the first generation of leaders supposed to witness? Peter said it over and over again in his speech: we saw the resurrected Jesus.

Theophilus, I say this because I heard from Peter and now pass on this testimony to you. We can trust the design and plan of God in establishing the Church—a body that truly is the supreme "act" of all the "acts" I wrote about in my book—because the first generation saw for themselves that Jesus was raised and they are passing on their testimony to us. This makes all the difference for the Church, even more than the signs or wonders or discipline or devotion. The fact that Jesus is alive and animates the whole thing means that the Church is never a movement of self-generation or ambition or simply an organized religion. Jesus also lives in the testimony of Peter and the Twelve, and he lives in what you say in support of that testimony.

> Acts 2:32 "This Jesus God raised up, and of that we all are witnesses."

1. Do I believe what Peter says? Why or why not? Who around me now faithfully affirms the words of Peter about Jesus?

2. How do I pass on this testimony? How does this testimony address my current life circumstances? How can I improve my transmission of Peter's words?

## Repent and Be Baptized

Peter's words hit a nerve among the people who listened, now swelled to 3000 souls. Jesus was present not only in his words, but in the hearts of the audience. They knew that they had to do something—not so much as to join something as change something. They recognized that they needed to change themselves before God.

Peter gave them a two-step response to his testimony about Jesus: First, they needed to repent for sin, which brings the promise of forgiveness. Then comes baptism, involving a decision to change, a ritual that started with John the Baptist and represents a fundamental decision to make a change in life. Baptism signifies the agreement to take steps to live a reformed life. This second step especially lays hold of Jesus alive and hidden within us as a resource for change. And the result of Peter's speech was that people decided to identify with the Church in Jerusalem.

Now I know, Theophilus, that this two-step process may sound foreign to your Greek neighbors and friends, but it is how one accepts what God began doing among the Jewish people, the ones to whom Jesus came first. You will hear me speak of this process in many of the accounts that I

14

will soon review with you—repentance and baptism into a new way of life is typical of what the Twelve taught in Jerusalem; and it is typical of what others like Philip and Paul practiced in their missions.

Peter's words led 3000 people to believe in Jesus. Peter knew that his words were simply the fulfillment of what Jesus had said before he ascended, that we would be witnesses. The people who were in front of him, the 3000 Pentecost pilgrims from Jerusalem, Judea, and from all over the world, well, they were the first to hear the testimony.

Then Peter said his message applied to the families—the "children"— of his audience. That means, he knew that these souls were connected to families and communities wherever they were from. Think about the worldwide impact of this speech, and then think about the power of any word you speak, Theophilus, and speak the word that is not just for your listener, but for the throngs that are connected to you through this listener.

Finally he said it spoke to those who were "far off every one whom the Lord our God calls to him." I don't know if Peter even dreamed of how "far off" his words would travel, but he must have remembered what Jesus said on the mountain about being witnesses in Jerusalem, Judea, Samaria, and then the ends of the earth. Those who were far off points to the Gentiles, and you should look into this connection by looking at the words of Isaiah and how it underlines what Peter quoted from the prophet Joel about the Spirit poured out on "all flesh." So by now you realize, Theophilus, that the Gentiles share in the Kingdom promise originally given to the Jews.

> Acts 2:37–39  **37** Now when they heard this they were cut to the heart, and said to Peter and the rest of the apostles, "Brethren, what shall we do?"  **38** And Peter said to them, "Repent, and be baptized every one of you in the name of Jesus Christ for the forgiveness of your sins; and you shall receive the gift of the Holy Spirit.  **39** For the promise is to you and to your children and to all that are far off, every one whom the Lord our God calls to him."

1. Where am I in my relationship with Jesus? Is there any sin in my life that I need to repent of and be forgiven?

2. How have I resolved to change? How is this change connected to my commitment to the Church?

3. How have I invested my words, my testimony, and my lifestyle in influencing others? How willing am I to be countercultural in my customs,

lifestyle, friends, and social connections? Which of these needs to be improved to serve me as a witness?

## The Lord Adds to the Church

Now the simple question I have for you, Theophilus: to what is the Lord adding those who respond to our testimony? What I have said here and in all of my accounts is that they naturally want to learn more about Jesus through even more listening to the testimony of Peter and the Twelve, then—by extension—to you and me. The continuation of the work of Jesus is what God does, and this continuation means that the Church grows. What is the normal life of the Church? I will let you go back and look at how Peter and the Twelve organized things—not just teaching, but a common life and sharing resources and community meals. All of this is also what Jesus himself is doing through all of us.

> Acts 2:47 And the Lord added to their number day by day those who were being saved.

1. Should I be praying for the Lord to add souls to the Church? Why or why not? Am I convinced that he is the one who saves? How sufficient do I believe his saving power is?

2. How am I connected to Peter's and the Twelve's testimony?

# Chapter 3

## "Acta" toward the Disqualified

What I write about the Twelve and their "acts" parallels what the Roman government tells us about the policies and laws of the emperors. That is, once Caesar sets something in place, it continues to hold sway even after the emperor is dead and gone. In Latin this legal term is called *acta*, and the idea is to keep the empire irreversibly progressing. Similarly, here I am trying to show you what the Apostles intended as *acta* so that you can build on the foundation they established.

I want to tell you now about the beginnings of the Apostles' new policy toward what Jews would consider outsiders, an *actus* that reverberates even now to you and me, Theophilus. The Twelve and all those in fellowship with them lived out their lives in faithfulness to the covenant of Abraham, Isaac, and Jacob. Their understanding was that the Kingdom Jesus announced benefited the Jews, and so the Twelve made it their aim to be faithful to their previous customs as understood from the Scriptures. In fact, however, it was one of their treasured customs that led Peter—and eventually all the Apostles—into a dramatic and surprising new understanding of how the Kingdom might include the broader Gentile world.

One day Peter and John encounter a man so disabled from birth that he had to be carried every day by his friends to the entrance of the temple, at the place everyone simply calls "Beautiful Gate." At this strategic location he would beg for money from passersby. This gate separates the area open to Gentiles from the area of the Jewish women.

Let me call attention to the details that may have escaped you earlier. Like many of their fellow Jerusalem residents, Peter and John had walked this way many times in the past to participate in the afternoon sacrifice service called *Minhah*. Every day they would pass this man at the gate and think nothing of it. This gate, separating areas open to the unclean and the next area open to women, was as far as he could go. He was a deformed man who did not have equal access with other Jews to the inner courtyards. Sad, inexplicable to outsiders, but these are the holiness protocols followed by temple authorities.

This time, however, Peter fixes his gaze on him in the same way that he had contemplated Jesus as he ascended from the Mount of Olives, just a few days earlier. Peter saw something deeper than before in this encounter. The crippled man represented not just an opportunity for physical healing but for the access of countless souls otherwise disqualified by their born identities. This was the beginning of a significant *actus*, Theophilus, which you will later recognize when Peter meets with Cornelius, a Roman centurion and a Gentile.

Peter solemnly invoked the name of Jesus, clasped the man's right hand, then summoned him to rise up: 'Come out of the born identity that holds you back! This name "Jesus" breaks the taboos and the restrictions that makes you unworthy and inferior.'

Peter's solemn reference to Jesus, you might say, was like swearing in the name of Caesar for Roman citizens. Only this time, it is no mere orator's flourish or politician's rhetoric. The man does get up, and now he jumps up and down. Imagine, he had never walked in his life! Then, for the first time in his life, he joins in the procession of fellow Jerusalemites going through the gate. After prayers with the priest at the hour of *Minhah*, he returns exhilarated and still healed. No wonder he leaps and shouts on the way out of the hallowed grounds!

> Acts 3:1–8 [1]Now Peter and John were going up to the temple at the hour of prayer, the ninth hour. [2] And a man lame from birth was being carried, whom they laid daily at that gate of the temple which is called Beautiful to ask alms of those who entered the temple. [3] Seeing Peter and John about to go into the temple, he asked for alms. [4] And Peter directed his gaze at him, with John, and said, "Look at us." [5] And he fixed his attention upon them, expecting to receive something from them. [6] But Peter said, "I have no silver and gold, but I give you what I have; in the name of Jesus Christ of Nazareth, walk." [7] And he took him by the right hand and raised him up; and immediately his feet and ankles were made strong. [8] And leaping up he stood and walked and entered the temple with them, walking and leaping and praising God.

1. How do I participate in a schedule of prayer in the course of the day?

2. How much power does the name of Jesus have in my life?

3. What kind of things do I think disqualify me from access to God?

4. What problems or situations have I given up on because they never seem to improve? How does this story inspire me to overcome impediments and restrictions in prayer?

## Message for the Jews

Now the man's new status is like a sensation for all the citizens: they remember that the man had always sat at the entrance to their court. When Peter walks back outside, a throng of fellow Jews follow him and the healed man. It is a ready-made opportunity for Peter to tell thousands about what this miracle has shown him about the presence of Jesus and expanding the Kingdom. First of all, he addresses the gathering crowd corporately and inclusively as "fellow Israelites." Why such a broad term? He sees himself addressing the whole nation—not just those present.

And then he explains the power of the name of Jesus, how this man's blessing somehow expresses the whole authority of the Kingdom promised from of old to Israel. While the full implications are yet to be seen, something powerful has happened and Peter is witness to it.

He calls them all to repent so that they can be forgiven for their history of unfaithfulness and especially for their rejection of Jesus himself. Then they as a people would experience seasons of revival (I call such periods καιροὶ ἀναψύξεως, *kairoi anapsucheōs*) from God. After a time of such favor toward the Jews, Peter promises that things would culminate in the restoration of their place in the divine plan for the world. He implies that the Jews were called by God not just for themselves but for the plan of God concerning those who were not Jews. Everything prophesied in the sacred scrolls—think Jeremiah, Isaiah, and Ezekiel—would come to pass. This last point brought the necessity for Peter's invocation of the name of Jesus. He may have been starting to realize that Israel was connected to the nations and not irreparably separated, that Jesus was extending salvation to "outsiders."

> Acts 3:19–21 **19** "Repent therefore, and turn again, that your sins may be blotted out, that times of refreshing may come from the presence of the Lord, **20** and that he may send the Christ

appointed for you, Jesus, **21** whom heaven must receive until the time for establishing all that God spoke by the mouth of his holy prophets from of old."

1. How does the Lord bring me into a season of renewal as I live as his disciple?

2. Describe what my revival might look like or what it might feel like. Does it permit me to have easier access to the Lord in prayer? Do I experience more forgiveness and divine acceptance? Why or why not?

3. What is it that we can expect the Lord to "establish" when Jesus returns "on the clouds"? In other words, what are some of the things that the prophets have predicted?

## Implications to Come

Peter concluded his speech by saying the plan of God came first of all to Israel—but now the blessing of Abraham would pass on to the world through Jesus. No one could predict how this *actus* would be fulfilled, and it would lie dormant for some weeks yet. Still, Theophilus, the Almighty had ordained it.

It was at first only a glimmer of something radical and new in the Kingdom. And the drama of the healing—a crippled man leaping and shouting—disguised it from everyone at first, not just you. Peter would later speak to a Roman named Cornelius and to his entire entourage about Jesus. Peter and Cornelius were both praying at this very *Minhah* hour in union with the priests, and they both find a "remembrance" or favor before God for the full implication of the cripple's healing. Let me continue my review with you through some questions.

> Acts 3:24–26 **24** "And all the prophets who have spoken, from Samuel and those who came afterwards, also proclaimed these days. **25** You are the sons of the prophets and of the covenant which God gave to your fathers, saying to Abraham, 'And in your posterity shall all the families of the earth be blessed.' **26** God, having raised up his servant, sent him to you first, to bless you in turning every one of you from your wickedness."

1. What are some of the prophecies that Peter refers to when he speaks about the days of Jesus and the Church?

2. How do the "sons of the prophets and of the covenant" bless what the Church has spread of the Kingdom?

3. Do I pray for a season of refreshment for the whole Church? How do I pray for the Jewish people?

# Chapter 4

## The Galileans and the Elites

Remember, men like Peter and most of his unvarnished companions were not native Judeans or cosmopolitan members of the Diaspora. Just days ago the angels on the Mount of Olives called them "Galileans," and their manners and speech clearly marked them as rustics. Yet the fact that something so dramatic occurred—imagine, a man born a total invalid, carried about by sympathetic benefactors, now bouncing about and shouting!—this could not be hidden or ignored. By the time Peter returned to give his speech, there were more than 5000 people present. Even the temple authorities, a group of Jewish leaders called the Sadducees, took note and threw out some dire implications for the temple if these Galilean teachings were advanced. They had to do something. So the best they could come up with was to lock up both the Apostles and their beneficiary, the healed man. They needed to strategize to contain this movement, so bizarrely breaking out from these uneducated simpletons.

One other point to notice about these Galilean rustics now addressing all of Israel. They were setting themselves up as teachers in the eyes of the Sadducees, thus they were considered as upstarts and rivals in the temple precincts. How could such men, uneducated and so unvarnished, stand with such boldness before thousands and speak with such poise?

> Acts 4:1–4 **1** And as they were speaking to the people, the priests and the captain of the temple and the Sadducees came upon them, **2** annoyed because they were teaching the people and proclaiming in Jesus the resurrection from the dead. **3** And they arrested them and put them in custody until the morrow, for it was already evening. 4 But many of those who heard the word believed; and the number of the men came to about five thousand.

1. How have I allowed my sense of inadequacy to keep me quiet about what I believe to be the truth?

2. Can I remember a time when my conviction about right and wrong motivated me to make a stand? How was my position different from prevailing opinion? For what cause would I be willing to stand up today? What forces would oppose me?

## Boldness

The Greek word that I used to describe their public position was παρρησία (*parrēsia*), a word associated with a citizen's courage to address the assembly as a member equal in standing to everyone else. Boldness borders on impudence and arrogance, because it implies that ordinary folks are claiming equality with the gifted and the high-born. But what is this Athenian principle in the face of the divinely endowed priesthood claimed by the Jerusalem temple authorities? Yet I can tell you as one who knows Paul, the missionary and Apostle you will meet later in my account, *parrēsia* ("boldness") is the quality that he would look for among his travelling companions and helpers.[1] He would seek out such pluck from fellow disciples.

A lot of other things grated against the elites and their henchmen who arrested Peter. First of all, it was evident that the Galilean followers of Jesus believed he was "messiah," a title that most of the Sadducean teachers and priests did not put stock in. What made it even worse was that their teaching about Jesus supported the doctrine of resurrection from the dead, another concept rejected by the Sadducees.

The Sadducean claim about messiah and resurrection is that they are not found in the writings or traditions—they do not accept any oral interpretations outside of Mosaic teachings. Moreover, Peter's words relied on many passages from the prophetic books, rejected by many temple authorities. As you struggle both to gather the sacred scrolls and to understand their teaching, Theophilus, keep in mind that for the Sadducees and Samaritans, only the Torah or Pentateuch (Genesis, Exodus, Leviticus, Numbers, and Deuteronomy) is authoritative.

> Acts 4:13–14 **13** Now when they saw the boldness of Peter and John, and perceived that they were uneducated, common men, they wondered; and they recognized that they had been with Jesus.

1. Cf. 2 Cor 3:12, 7:4; Eph 3:12, 6:19.

**14** But seeing the man that had been healed standing beside them, they had nothing to say in opposition.

1. Put yourself in Peter's shoes. Would you be ready to make such a stand?

2. On what ground in my life as a Christian would I make my defense of Jesus?

3. What does it mean to be bold? Can I think of any times in my life when I was bold? What made me be so willing to stand out?

4. Have I had an experience of Christ in me that is an inner resource for being bold? Describe how it was motivating.

## Futility

Peter and John remained unmoved by the Sadducees' show of force and follow-up threats. And the Sadducees realized that it is futile to lecture them about their lack of qualification for leadership. So they ordered the complete silencing of the Christian message. In fact, to quote them: The "whole business" is not even to be "uttered," much less "taught" (here is the Greek I used: τὸ καθόλου μὴ φθέγγεσθαι μηδὲ διδάσκειν, *to katholou mē phtheggesthai mēde didaskein*). And what is Peter and John's response? They fall back on their basic position: they have "seen and heard" something, and they cannot deny it. Again the preeminent position of the Apostles is that they are only witnessing, not developing grand strategies and theologies. The Sadducees refuse to compromise a single iota of their position: their immovable force runs into the irresistible object of the Apostles' testimony! Yet it is their institutional dominance over the temple teaching that soon will result in a juggernaut of opposition to the "Way" that the Apostles represent.

> Acts 4:18–20 **18** So they called them and charged them not to speak or teach at all in the name of Jesus. **19** But Peter and John answered them, "Whether it is right in the sight of God to listen to you rather than to God, you must judge; **20** for we cannot but speak of what we have seen and heard."

1. What is the prevailing view (perhaps the "politically correct" position) that I have to deal with regularly? What kind of objections and questions must I continually confront?

2. Does this prevailing view cause me to be intimidated? How? Can I maintain this simple testimony in the face of opposition? How am I pressured to maintain silence?

3. Do I find that I can "utter" a word of truth in such situations? How can I teach under these circumstances? Imagine and describe a situation where an utterance might be a gateway for teaching.

4. What have I seen and heard that keeps me zealous and faithful? What do I know through Peter and John and the apostolic witness they represent?

## Courage and Action

Theophilus, what would have been your response to the threats that came from the temple authorities and social elites? In spite of all their inadequacy and inexperience, the Twelve refused to give in. The "Way" they represented was not a Greek philosophy of the mind or intellect, nor was it an Asian mystery cult of emotion or cathartic experience, but courageous testimony about Jesus as risen from the dead and invisibly working through them.

In any event, the kind of response that Peter and John demonstrated is rare: most everyone these days accepts the "new imperial order" and avoids conflict rather than facing it head-on. I would call the Twelve's approach a manly response, one that I hope shakes every reader of my book out of complacency and apathy about this world order. How will you and I respond when the Status Quo repudiates what we stand for, the Kingdom? Will we slither away back to our own Galilees and whisper in secret what we know to be true? Will we relegate to the margins of Jerusalem or Rome what Jesus established as the absolute and final voice of authority? Rather than cave in, Peter and John faced things head-on and even went on the offensive. Their boldness and decisive action marks their response as "chesty" and challenging.

Peter and John's spirit was catchy for the Church in Jerusalem, so that now all those around the Apostles engaged in public witness to the Kingdom. This is the faith of the first generation of the Church, and I tell you about it here in hopes that it will fill you with confidence (*parrēsia*) as you read my book and as you give your own testimony.

The final picture I leave you with, Theophilus, is the corporate response of the believers in Jerusalem. Put yourself in their shoes: they were a ragtag band of souls, led by a bunch of outliers who were for the most part from backwoods Galilee. Under such pressure, you would have thought that they would have retreated. Instead they envisioned themselves in an age-old conflict between forces who stood for the Kingdom as beginning with David and those who stood against the Kingdom, all the priests and politicians who conspired against them.

They gather together to pray, and this is the gist of their prayer:

> Lord, we know the opposition that David faced when he established the kingdom of Israel. In the same way, Jesus faced a united front of enemies when he preached a restoration of the Kingdom to us. Today, this same plight faces us today, because we corporately represent Jesus at work among us. We are surrounded and threatened. Now help us—like you helped David and Jesus! Help us to do the same things as you did in your time of fellowship among us: healing, to love, to speak out boldly.

Step back and see how their prayer now extends to you and to every reader, Theophilus: a hostile reception awaits your witness, and in fact you may feel that "kings of the earth and the rulers take counsel against" you. These believers in Jerusalem were praying for you at that moment. It is not just about David, Jesus, or even the Jerusalem church! Be strong in your prayer and respond in a chesty way. That's the whole point: like my "unfinished tale," so their prayer is unfinished. Both reach out to you.

Don't compromise on the "whole business" (τὸ καθόλου, *to katholou*) passed on by the first generation in Jerusalem. I am not just speaking about the business of doctrines and teachings, but about healings, signs, and wonders. These things show that Jesus is at work among us though hidden—read again what I wrote. Just as Jesus was present when Peter took the hand of the cripple, now he will be present in others in similar and dramatic fashion. And you will soon see how Jesus is at work among other groups outside of the Twelve and outside of Judea.

One final point, Theophilus, before we move on. When the prayer ended, what happens? The ones who gathered in prayer experience another outpouring of the Spirit of Jesus like at Pentecost. This time, though, instead of a mighty wind, there was a shaking of the place where they were. Was it an earthquake? Here's my take: the decision that these men and women took was so profound within themselves, it was as if a primeval battle had been fought within the confines of their prayer. The results were so cosmic that it was as if a divine signature rested on their unity and intent. Jesus, who had disappeared in the clouds, now showed that he was still present among them by the shaking of the place.

Now I realize that the whole thing sounds like one of Aesop's fables. Is it a make-believe myth cooked up by naïve Galileans and reported to me to get you to imitate their boldness? I leave it to you to determine as you reread my book whether I am passing on an incredible riddle or a private joke. Only let me quote the next line in that particular Psalm that the believers prayed that day: "He who sits in the heavens laughs!" And, alas, to quote from Aesop, he will laugh last.

> Acts 4:23–31 [23] When they were released they went to their friends and reported what the chief priests and the elders had said to them. [24] And when they heard it, they lifted their voices together to God and said, "Sovereign Lord, who didst make the heaven and the earth and the sea and everything in them, [25] who by the mouth of our father David, thy servant, didst say by the Holy Spirit, 'Why did the Gentiles rage, and the peoples imagine vain things? [26] The kings of the earth set themselves in array, and the rulers were gathered together, against the Lord and against his Anointed'— [27] for truly in this city there were gathered together against thy holy servant Jesus, whom thou didst anoint, both Herod and Pontius Pilate, with the Gentiles and the peoples of Israel, [28] to do whatever thy hand and thy plan had predestined to take place. [29] And now, Lord, look upon their threats, and grant to thy servants to speak thy word with all boldness, [30] while thou stretchest out thy hand to heal, and signs and wonders are performed through the name of thy holy servant Jesus." [31] And when they had prayed, the place in which they were gathered together was shaken; and they were all filled with the Holy Spirit and spoke the word of God with boldness.

1. What levels of meaning can I recognize in the Psalm the believers in Jerusalem prayed? How can their use of Scripture energize how I read and pray the Bible?

2. How can I recognize that every passage of Scripture operates on various platforms of context? Find other passages where there are various

layers of meaning while incorporating the current moment in the loop of its application?

> *Prayer*: O Lord, help us to be courageous and bold in our witness, to face even death, with such boldness. Help us to see things more deeply and treasure what you reveal to us. Help us to heal, to love, and speak out.

## Tested by Fire

Brinksmanship brought the best out of the believers, as it will for you, Theophilus. Several weeks earlier Pentecost had brought together a large group of people who wanted to associate with the life of prayer and the teachings of the Apostles. It was easier then, because they were riding the crest of a powerful experience. Now the situation called for a counterculture to be built on the fundamental decision that Peter and John had made to witness and perform public acts in spite of the opposition of the elites in Jerusalem. If signs and wonders and healings reflected the presence of Jesus among the Apostles, now it was the community life and its culture that stood out to the external world as a testimony to his indwelling. There is a fantastic story to tell about how radical and urgent this first generation community was. The story illustrates how the community developed a counterculture based on transparency and unselfishness. In fact, really what was going on is that the Church was beginning to stand out even more than the Apostles. You will begin to notice this change in the rest of my book as I shift to speak about other representatives of the Kingdom of God—people like the "Seven," who were the so-called deacons, and eventually Paul. Even more than through the Twelve, the Church as a whole spread the message of Jesus from Jerusalem to Judea to Samaria and outward.

Meet Barnabas. He had come on pilgrimage from Cyprus so long ago, and by now was so transplanted in Jerusalem that he owned property in the city. When he witnessed what was going on among that first generation of believers, his good heart would not let him rest until he had made a total response. He sold one of his properties and made all the money available to the believers by laying the funds at the feet of the Apostles. This of course caused quite a sensation among the rest of the community who also began to make their personal possessions available to anyone who had need. All of a sudden it became de rigueur among the zealots in the Church.

Nothing like this had ever taken hold among the conventional residents of Jerusalem, though I am sure you have heard about other bohemian groups where you live who have decided to show allegiance to their offbeat causes by similar countercultural practices. Anyway, the whole thing took on a momentum all its own until everyone was talking about it.

Enter Ananias and his wife Sapphira. To gain attention and admiration, they imitated Barnabas by selling one of their properties; but they lacked Barnabas's good heart. They pilfered some of the money and profiled themselves as being as radical as anyone in their testimony to the Kingdom. What they did not reckon with was that the Kingdom of God is not something to be toyed with. It actually is God's, not a human organization that can be manipulated or fooled.

The result? Both man and wife were brought into a solemn hearing before everyone, Apostles and community, where they were struck dead because of their deception. Everyone walked away thinking now that they had just witnessed a divine court, where an all-knowing Judge had rendered a final verdict. Thus, the implication for that first generation in Jerusalem was that the community of believers, presided over by the Apostles, is a divine operation that corporately continues the work of Jesus to establish the Kingdom of God. And they all had to decide whether to unite radically with it or leave it—but not to have it both ways.

When I told you this story earlier, I was trying to clue you in on what a supernatural niche the Church occupies in the economy of salvation history. This of course goes back to the life of Jesus which I told you in my earlier book.

> Acts 4:36—5:2 **36** Thus Joseph who was surnamed by the apostles Barnabas (which means, Son of encouragement), a Levite, a native of Cyprus, **37** sold a field which belonged to him, and brought the money and laid it at the apostles' feet.
>
> **1**But a man named Ananias with his wife Sapphira sold a piece of property, **2** and with his wife's knowledge he kept back some of the proceeds, and brought only a part and laid it at the apostles' feet.

1. Have I ever witnessed what I believe to be divine judgment? Describe it. What kind of awe or fear did it generate in me? Did I decide to live my life differently as a result?

2. Can I tie the establishment of the Kingdom of God to human groups or organizations? Be specific about whether what Luke is telling Theophilus is also something I have witnessed for myself. Any parallels come to mind?

3. What is my assessment of the Church as a place of divine judgment? How does this grand view of the Jerusalem Church translate into my local church?

# Chapter 5

## Collision of Paradoxes

This chain of events set the Church and the Apostles on a collision course with the elites in Jerusalem. They had several days earlier been given an ultimatum, but they even more decidedly had committed themselves to following the "Way" of Jesus. So now the authorities in Jerusalem, gathered together in a council called the Sanhedrin—something like what you would call the βουλή (*boulē*)[1] in your area, except for the stronger religious identity of the Jewish members—and arrested all the Apostles.

Their strategy for containing the "Way"—the earliest name we were given—was to snuff out the Apostles, the eyewitnesses to Jesus, so that the movement would fizzle. While it makes sense, you can imagine how futile it was, given what I said above about the corporate investment of Jesus within the united witness of the believers. The Church by now is starting to awaken in its subsidiary parts, and to take a life of its own apart from its leaders.

And it was futile from the divine perspective too. For in the middle of the night, a miracle happened: somehow the Apostles slipped out and began teaching at daybreak in the temple once more. The Apostles said that an angel escorted them, but the guards stationed there and the solid prison doors brooked no such fantasy. At any rate, the Apostles made no attempt to evade owning up to their actions. Their feeling was that they had nothing to fear if God was in control.

As usual, Peter was targeted as the spokesman for the Apostles at the Sanhedrin proceedings. After all, he was the one that the Jerusalem elites had warned in the first place when he performed the miracle at the

---

1. A body of city fathers governing civic life for local jurisdictions, usually headed up by an administrative official called an "archon."

Beautiful Gate. Peter and John in that incident received the ultimatum to stop uttering and teaching τὸ καθόλου (*to katholou*) the whole business about Jesus and the Kingdom.

So Peter is back in the spotlight. Listen carefully to how he responds:

> "We must obey God rather than men. The God of our fathers raised Jesus whom you killed by hanging him on a tree. God exalted him at his right hand as Leader and Savior, to give repentance to Israel and forgiveness of sins. And we are witnesses to these things, and so is the Holy Spirit whom God has given to those who obey him."

This is a dense statement to unpack.

*"God of our fathers."* Peter is not speaking in his own name or authority, but he invokes, first, the pedigree of Israel. He means primarily the "fathers," the patrimony binding Jews together by the covenant.

Then he says, *"We are witnesses"* of repentance and forgiveness in Jesus. That is, the Apostles and the apostolic tradition now is Peter's basis for public testimony. Simply put, he means the community that is radically united in taking courageous steps along the "Way" of Jesus. That "Way" brings repentance and forgiveness.

*"So is the Holy Spirit."* Notice his final and ultimate authority, the Holy Spirit. This is a bold and audacious claim that made many illustrious men in the room wince. Who are the Apostles that they can identify the inspiration and guidance of the Holy Spirit? What is the "Church" compared to the long history of great assembly of the elders of Israel beginning with Ezra.[2] And who authorized the Church? What the Sanhedrin sees is a motley crew of outsiders from all walks of life, except of course from among the literati and sophisticates.

Moreover, who is Peter to make these claims? Peter has his own testimony to offer. He has known forgiveness when a short while ago he had denied Jesus publicly and more recently was rehabilitated. Presumably, Theophilus, you are acquainted with this incident from my first book and can recall some of the details surrounding his life story.

In this same vein of personal testimony, Peter also represents everyone who has received forgiveness and repentance. This more inclusive voice is surely at least part of what Peter means by the Holy Spirit serving as a witness before the Sanhedrin. Peter is representing every person who

---

2. The fundamental handbook of the Rabbis called the Mishnah claims its foundation in the succession of Jewish voices beginning with the Great Assembly (Ezra).

has committed to the Way—certainly you and me. And so he continues to speak about who we are.

And finally, in the strangest of paradoxes, the last reference to the Holy Spirit suggests that the Sanhedrin itself is a participant in the process because Peter does not limit this spiritualized recognition to the Apostles or the community of believers. He implies that even the Sanhedrin partakes in this Holy Spirit chain of communication, perhaps unawares. There is no better proof than the unwitting prophecy that comes next in my account, namely, the words that Gamaliel speaks about what to do about the Apostles in their custody. Gamaliel realizes the futility of snuffing out this movement, if it is of God.

Surely Gamaliel's utterance is no different than the prophecy that Caiaphas delivered about Jesus just before his death: it is better that one man die for the people.[3] How did Caiaphas speak except by the Holy Spirit? When you and I speak boldly our testimony, we prompt a response that reverberates until even unyielding opposition is drowned out.

Thus, when Peter refers to the Holy Spirit in his speech, he means it as a corporate operation, that we might apply to all of the diverse levels that Peter mentions. The context that the Apostles, Peter, all the believers, and even the Sanhedrin must obey God rather than man suggests that Holy Spirit is the final advocate for the unfailing sovereignty of the Almighty. The Holy Spirit stands alongside the whole process to give the affirmation that Peter is right in what he is saying.

God is often at work quite outside our reach, orchestrating events and human hearts. Sometimes he works even through "enemies" and frustrates their efforts. Sometimes he works through people that we previously thought were "enemies," but who are obedient to the Spirit of Jesus in their own way. The Holy Spirit penetrates beyond our deepest searching, and we need to recognize that he will surprise us in the day when our own missionary efforts have fallen short or seem to have failed. On that day, we will thrill to see how God has completed our efforts to bring all things into divine subjection, using even things which are inconsistent with our common sensibilities.

When the verdict is given, there is yet another surprise: Adversities and persecutions bring joy. The persecution and suffering bring joy. Theophilus, I did not mean that the beating or the calumny that the Apostles received somehow satisfied some perverse masochistic desire.

---

3. Assuming that Theophilus was aware of what John 11:50 records.

No, every human being has an instinct for self-preservation and naturally cringes at the treatment the Apostles received. Nonetheless a supernatural joy envelops the Apostles and marks anyone who is born of God. To be dishonored because of our association with Jesus sets us apart from everything else, as if we are metamorphosed into his own extended self. As such, we then become, as it were, a reverse target for God: divine love and grace is poured out on us because we are consecrated alongside of prophets, priests, the temple, and pleasing sacrifices. We fulfill a role that Jesus played when he too was set apart for God's purpose at his baptism. While earmarked for suffering, nonetheless he knew an incipient contentment shared with the Eternal One. So close was the bonding that it was organic, a father-son identity harking back to the original creation of Adam: "This is my beloved Son in whom I am very pleased." Go back and review what I said about this event in my first book.

> Acts 5:27–32 27 And when they had brought them, they set them before the council. And the high priest questioned them, 28 saying, "We strictly charged you not to teach in this name, yet here you have filled Jerusalem with your teaching and you intend to bring this man's blood upon us." 29 But Peter and the apostles answered, "We must obey God rather than men. 30 The God of our fathers raised Jesus whom you killed by hanging him on a tree. 31 God exalted him at his right hand as Leader and Savior, to give repentance to Israel and forgiveness of sins. 32 And we are witnesses to these things, and so is the Holy Spirit whom God has given to those who obey him."

> Acts 5:38–42 38 "So in the present case I tell you, keep away from these men and let them alone; for if this plan or this undertaking is of men, it will fail; 39 but if it is of God, you will not be able to overthrow them. You might even be found opposing God!" 40 So they took his advice, and when they had called in the apostles, they beat them and charged them not to speak in the name of Jesus, and let them go. 41 Then they left the presence of the council, rejoicing that they were counted worthy to suffer dishonor for the name. 42 And every day in the temple and at home they did not cease teaching and preaching Jesus as the Christ.

1. Explain in your own words how Peter believes he is simply a link in a chain of divine communication? Can I think of any parallels or practical illustrations to this process?

2. How do I hear what God is asking me to do? What makes me persist in doing God's will, even when there is opposition?

3. How do I pray for such outcomes among public leaders and authorities, even when they do not favorably receive the Lord or the Way?

4. Have I ever experienced joy that seems to come inexplicably when I am under pressure? How did it change my perspective?

# Chapter 6

## The Seven

The Apostles locked up in prison and immobilized from mission only opens up opportunities for new reinforcements to take their place. One group of illustrious recruits was the Seven. If the Twelve represents the macrocosm of Israel in its completeness as the twelve tribes of Israel, the Seven represents the microcosm of Israel, in its local and practical dimensions.

How does the Seven show this? Whenever Jews find themselves together outside of Jerusalem, they always begin reconstituting themselves through an assembly of seven select men. These men set up necessary communal functions, charity and relief, policy-making, and routines.

In this case, the group I call the Seven was summoned to help in administration. You can imagine that big problems emerged as several thousand new people started meeting regularly for teaching and prayer. The first generation Jerusalem leaders passed on the torch of their testimony to the Seven and gave them practical responsibilities. Yet, as things unfolded, it turns out that they operated with autonomy in an ad-hoc way that vastly outstripped their practical responsibilities. In effect, their calling served as a pathway for the Kingdom to burst forth in new and powerful ways. Clearly these men already had shown ability and calling—thus, we call them simply the Seven.

The preeminent member of the Seven was Stephen. His spiritual aptitude and fearlessness took him well beyond the task assigned to him by the Apostles, namely, the distribution of relief, and entangled him in disputes with Sanhedrin vigilantes. The rationale of these hyper-loyalists was that if the Twelve could not be stopped because of their public stature, perhaps the Seven newly commissioned agents of the Way could.

So the opposition dragged Stephen in front of the Sanhedrin for an emergency session, before anyone could martial much counterevidence. Nonetheless, as I mentioned earlier, it is futile to fight divine realities, invisible but close at hand. I used a word, ἀτενίζω (*atenizō*), in my account to describe how the Sanhedrin looked at Stephen. You may remember this word from my description of Jesus ascending on the Mount of Olives, when the disciples were trying to grasp the departure of Jesus Christ from the world, when he ascended into the clouds. I take the word to mean "see with clarity" or even "see with inward vision."

Here the crowd gazes deeply into Stephen's face and intuitively recognizes a strangely angelic mien. As you know, angels always look upon the face of God, and so are radiant in divine glory. Did bystanders think that Stephen was caught up in an angel's beatific vision so that his face showed an infused glow? Maybe. I am simply suggesting that heavenly glory was tangibly close to everyone present in this confrontation. For angels, time and tension and even sin—at least the way we now have the ability to choose for it—mean nothing; all that matters is surrender—and the angels themselves can do nothing other. In their case, glory is both fearful and beautiful: it dances on a knife-edge of all-consuming holiness or all-transforming grace. For humans, the choice to receive the grace of such a moment is freely offered, but—alas—the Sanhedrin voted with its feet to reject this propitious moment.

> Acts 6:3–6 **3**"Therefore, brethren, pick out from among you seven men of good repute, full of the Spirit and of wisdom, whom we may appoint to this duty. **4** But we will devote ourselves to prayer and to the ministry of the word." **5** And what they said pleased the whole multitude, and they chose Stephen, a man full of faith and of the Holy Spirit, and Philip, and Prochorus, and Nicanor, and Timon, and Parmenas, and Nicolaus, a proselyte of Antioch. **6** These they set before the apostles, and they prayed and laid their hands upon them.

> Acts 6:15 And gazing at him, all who sat in the council saw that his face was like the face of an angel.

1. How do I approach my daily duties and responsibilities? Do I allow for the breaking forth of grace and glory as I do them?

2. Have there ever been times when I have observed drama or charisma so intense that time seemed to stand still or that I was transported elsewhere? Try to recall them and describe them.

3. Have I ever been so drawn into the divine presence that circumstances around me did not matter? Bring the situation(s) back to mind for recollection. Have I ever noticed this state in others?

4. How might have this condition have helped Stephen makes his defense?

## Stephen's Testimony a Failure?

Stephen senses a pivotal moment for the work of Jesus, for his audience sees him as an angel, a messenger. I don't know how to calculate the effects of Stephen's speech. It is not an easy one to follow in terms of its logical progression or lucidity. He reviewed a few biographical sketches that come from the annals of Israel's history. In each of these stories he uncovered vestiges of divine intervention that were at first insignificant and unpromising. Instead he hinted that divine fulfillment is executed over long periods and in diverse ways. For example, you may be familiar with Abraham and how the divine plan for a homeland and offspring tarried.

Another hero, Joseph: agonizing and measly were the returns of his faith experiences. First, he languished as a slave and a prisoner; and then even after an amazing rescue from Pharaoh's prison, all that happened by the end of his life was the provision of refuge for his family, hardly the boast of a national champion. Yes, his father Jacob returned to Canaan, the land promised to him in his youth, but only as a corpse and then only to as much land as his grave required.

And surely you know Moses, his next example. He began life as an infant abandoned to the stark forces of Mother Nature and fickle chance—and then lived life in relative obscurity in the courts of Pharaoh's daughter. For all of the apparent prodigies that surrounded him in fragmentary ways, the people for whom he had come did not recognize his claim and his destiny as a national savior. Neither did his kinfolk have any idea that they were called and chosen. The result were forty years of oblivion and obscurity for him, years when one would have thought he would be most productive. Then even after Moses succeeded in leading the people out of Egypt, they still ended up rejecting their divine election.

This litany of failures makes me ask, What is the point of Stephen's last words, his last chance to tell the world about the purpose of his life? There were some glimmers of insight that his speech gave me about what to live for, but for the most part I can only guess what his real point was. The apparent result was the mob assembled at the hearing was enraged, and made quick business out of snatching and stoning him.

I suppose you could say that his fleeting reference to the hard-heartedness of the people toward the prophets sent to them was only confirmed in what happened to Stephen, their present victim. The climactic blow in his speech was his indictment of temple. This was the final straw for an audience of Sanhedrin partisans. No wonder the mob erupts into utter pandemonium at Stephen's words.

One thing I know: there was one person in the crowd who proves that God's ways are often inscrutable paradoxes that beggar what I can write in words. His name was Saul. The fact that the whole audience was swept away into murderous fury does not negate the fact that the very one who might have incited their violent outburst also seems to have been moved by Stephen's oration. The killers laid their garments at Saul's feet; but what was germinating in Saul's heart as he looked upon the face of an angel? What holiness unleashed in the crowd's rage, did grace transform in this soul? Is this another case where he who sits in the heavens laughs?

Let me offer another reflection on Stephen's speech. Was his martyrdom a demonstration of his message? If Abraham did not see the results of his obedience, if Joseph's returns were meager, if Moses labored only for rejection, what can we say about Stephen's climactic flash in the last of his allotted breaths on earth? Perhaps his undoing only punctuates the message of his final testament: even in death, glory reverberates and achieves its crescendo. The success of Stephen's life and speech ultimately depends on its impact on people like Saul—and you and me, Theophilus. The divine riddle now is sprung upon the audience.

And about Stephen himself, what can I say of these last few moments? Stephen is transfixed by another world than the one before him. He sees this reality hidden from the angry mob; he too "gazes on" it—and so he has the face of an angel beholding the glory of God. Once the Apostles peered at Jesus in like manner as he disappeared into the clouds. Now Stephen contemplates Jesus who makes a special appearance to him, to congratulate him for a testimony well-given. The one seated in heaven has the last laugh and now rises to welcome Stephen.

Thus received, Stephen's final form metamorphoses into Jesus redivivus[1] and simultaneously Adam *imago dei:*[2] he forgives his killers as Jesus did before dying. That is to say, Adam and Jesus are summed up in Stephen. How will you and I die, Theophilus? Will others see in this our final act an analogy of the Second Adam's relationship with humanity?

Acts 7:4–6 **4** "Then he departed from the land of the Chaldeans, and lived in Haran. And after his father died, God removed him from there into this land in which you are now living; **5** yet he gave him no inheritance in it, not even a foot's length, but promised to give it to him in possession and to his posterity after him, though he had no child. **6** And God spoke to this effect, that his posterity would be aliens in a land belonging to others, who would enslave them and ill-treat them four hundred years."

Acts 7:9 "And the patriarchs, jealous of Joseph, sold him into Egypt; but God was with him."

Acts 7:15–16 **15**"Jacob went down into Egypt. And he died, himself and our fathers, **16** and they were carried back to Shechem and laid in the tomb that Abraham had bought for a sum of silver from the sons of Hamor in Shechem."

Acts 7:27–30 **27** "But the man who was wronging his neighbor thrust him aside, saying, 'Who made you a ruler and a judge over us? **28** Do you want to kill me as you killed the Egyptian yesterday?' **29** At this retort Moses fled, and became an exile in the land of Midian, where he became the father of two sons. **30** Now when forty years had passed, an angel appeared to him in the wilderness of Mount Sinai, in a flame of fire in a bush."

Acts 7:35 "This Moses whom they refused, saying, 'Who made you a ruler and a judge?' God sent as both ruler and deliverer by the hand of the angel that appeared to him in the bush."

Acts 7:39–41 **39** "Our fathers refused to obey him, but thrust him aside, and in their hearts they turned to Egypt, **40** saying to Aaron,

1. "Alive again" in Latin—sometimes used of the prophets among Jews or emperors among Romans.

2. "The image of God"—used to describe the creation of the human being in Gen 1:26–27, then used in Christian contexts to describe the divine intention for the perfection of Adam. Luke himself favors the connection of Adam and Jesus in his unique genealogy (Luke 3:23–38).

'Make for us gods to go before us; as for this Moses who led us out from the land of Egypt, we do not know what has become of him.' **41** And they made a calf in those days, and offered a sacrifice to the idol and rejoiced in the works of their hands."

Acts 7:51–52 **51** "You stiff-necked people, uncircumcised in heart and ears, you always resist the Holy Spirit. As your fathers did, so do you. **52** Which of the prophets did not your fathers persecute? And they killed those who announced beforehand the coming of the Righteous One, whom you have now betrayed and murdered. . . ."

Acts 7:55–59 **55** But he, full of the Holy Spirit, gazed into heaven and saw the glory of God, and Jesus standing at the right hand of God; **56** and he said, "Behold, I see the heavens opened, and the Son of man standing at the right hand of God." **57** But they cried out with a loud voice and stopped their ears and rushed together upon him. **58** Then they cast him out of the city and stoned him; and the witnesses laid down their garments at the feet of a young man named Saul. **59** And as they were stoning Stephen, he prayed, "Lord Jesus, receive my spirit."

1. Who are God's choices for leadership and change in these passages?

2. How is grace and favor at work in their lives? How was worldly failure also at work?

3. How were they unrecognized by human beings around them?

4. Have I ever despaired of seeing the fruit of faithful action only to be surprised later by what effects my own deeds have accomplished? Call them to mind and give thanks.

5. Go back over the last paragraph of Luke's retelling and try to answer Luke's questions at the end.

Acts 8:1–4 **1** And Saul was consenting to his death. And on that day a great persecution arose against the church in Jerusalem; and they were all scattered throughout the region of Judea and Samaria, except the apostles. **2** Devout men buried Stephen, and made great lamentation over him. **3** But Saul was ravaging the church, and entering house after house, he dragged off men and women and committed them to prison. **4** Now those who were scattered went about preaching the word.

# Chapter 7

## Fairy Tale or Furies?

You can lay to rest any notion of fairy-tale bliss as we waited for the "times of renewal" that were promised. Clearly the Holy Spirit had allowed tribulations to dog us as the Way expanded. The profile and relative popularity of the Twelve made them a harder target to bring down. They were the first ones for authorities to go after, then it was Stephen, and finally there was harassing and stalking against the rank and file believers.

Yet the reverse also was true: people like Saul were the target of testimony and prayer. Saul was not the only target for Stephen's testimony. The Way itself now was forced to buck the centripetal winds propelling it toward Jerusalem and the Apostles and ride on centrifugal winds whipping it into surrounding lands for the first time. In other words, we were pioneering new frontiers, places we could have only imagined just a few short weeks ago.

The Furies were unleashed; but the harder they panted after us, the more elusive became their aim of containing the Kingdom of God. Let this be a lesson to you, Theophilus, the very point of Gamaliel's prophecy to the Sanhedrin: if something comes from God, no force can shut it down.

And yet, from the Church's point of view, the Furies also brought risk and danger. It was a strange way to fulfill Peter's prophetic word after the man born lame was healed. He had said that "times of revival" would come upon those who repented and converted. Peter did not mean periods of bliss where there was no hardship or persecution. Quite the contrary. Remember what happened just after he announced these times: the Apostles were arrested and summoned to court, followed by Stephen's martyrdom. The Twelve were temporarily spared further retributions, but the outburst of violence now pummeled the rank and file of the Church.

42

Still, the Kingdom sallied forth unabashed, and we found a time of courage. There is no better example than Philip, one of the members of the illustrious Seven. With the persecution in full swing, Philip left from Jerusalem and took his testimony to the periphery of Judea where he met whole peoples we had never before envisioned within the Kingdom.

How does one man have such influence that whole peoples and even nations repent and convert? Philip was not squeamish about advancing into the land of the Samaritans. There he shows the kind of works that we had associated with the Apostles, namely, healing and preaching.

The Samaritans are always on the lookout for wonderworkers, for they are always searching for a prophet like Moses to arise. For them, the proof of Moses' (or anyone's) divine calling is the performance of miracles.

So amazing are these things that Philip performs in the public eye that he rivets the attention of a man called Simon. Simon already traffics in the world of magic and miracles, and many Samaritans consider him a channel of supernatural power. By now, rumors have reached me that that he showboats about Mediterranean lands, and is ballyhooed with honors and acclaim wherever he goes. It is even said that Rome itself is so enthralled with his claim to be an emanation of the gods that they have commissioned a statue and an inscription in his honor.[1] When Philip arrives in Samaria, Simon begins to lose his audience.

The Samaritan faith has its own peculiarity in relation to the Jewish faith, and I won't get into the nitty-gritty of its teachings. Suffice it to say, the Samaritans are familiar with much of what Philip preaches, especially since the Kingdom of God is so evident in the miracles they see. Even Simon the magician goes along with Philip—at least temporarily.

All this takes place through a member of the Seven, and the news echoes back to Jerusalem. The Apostles send out Peter and John to check out how compatible this mission is to what the Church stands for. The Samaritans are often marginalized and despised by Jews—though close enough to them that I do not rule Samaritans out as Israelites. Philip and the Samaritans show the same signs of Jesus invisibly at work among them as the first generation of leaders saw in Jerusalem. Peter and John give their blessing to this surprising expansion, the first one outside of Jerusalem. It is, however, exactly what Jesus predicted just before he ascended: we are

---

1. Justin Martyr, *First Apology* 26.2–5; Irenaeus, *Against Heresies* 1.23.1; Tertullian, *Apology* 13.9.

witnesses, he said, to Jerusalem, to Samaria, and then to the ends of the earth.

Acts 8:5–25 5 Philip went down to a city of Samaria, and proclaimed to them the Christ. 6 And the multitudes with one accord gave heed to what was said by Philip, when they heard him and saw the signs which he did. 7 For unclean spirits came out of many who were possessed, crying with a loud voice; and many who were paralyzed or lame were healed. 8 So there was much joy in that city. 9 But there was a man named Simon who had previously practiced magic in the city and amazed the nation of Samaria, saying that he himself was somebody great. 10 They all gave heed to him, from the least to the greatest, saying, "This man is that power of God which is called Great." 11 And they gave heed to him, because for a long time he had amazed them with his magic. 12 But when they believed Philip as he preached good news about the kingdom of God and the name of Jesus Christ, they were baptized, both men and women. 13 Even Simon himself believed, and after being baptized he continued with Philip. And seeing signs and great miracles performed, he was amazed. 14 Now when the apostles at Jerusalem heard that Samaria had received the word of God, they sent to them Peter and John, 15 who came down and prayed for them that they might receive the Holy Spirit; 16 for it had not yet fallen on any of them, but they had only been baptized in the name of the Lord Jesus. 17 Then they laid their hands on them and they received the Holy Spirit. 18 Now when Simon saw that the Spirit was given through the laying on of the apostles' hands, he offered them money, 19 saying, "Give me also this power, that any one on whom I lay my hands may receive the Holy Spirit." 20 But Peter said to him, "Your silver perish with you, because you thought you could obtain the gift of God with money! 21 You have neither part nor lot in this matter, for your heart is not right before God. 22 Repent therefore of this wickedness of yours, and pray to the Lord that, if possible, the intent of your heart may be forgiven you. 23 For I see that you are in the gall of bitterness and in the bond of iniquity." 24 And Simon answered, "Pray for me to the Lord, that nothing of what you have said may come upon me." 25 Now when they had testified and spoken the word of the Lord, they returned to Jerusalem, preaching the gospel to many villages of the Samaritans.

1. Have I ever experienced a "season of revival" exactly when what I was doing for God was difficult and even rejected? How did I maintain my cool? How did God open up new doors for me because of my stand?

2. How does persecution actually stimulate growth in the Kingdom of God?

3. How does the work of Philip, one of the Seven, compare to those of the Twelve?

4. Think about any "Samaritans" in my life that I have not helped because of my disapproval of what they represent or because of the challenges they raise. Pray for new ways of reaching out to them.

# Chapter 8

## Advance into Ethiopia?

Samaria secured by the Apostles' approval, yet another major initiative is in store for Philip before he settles down in life. An angel appears to Philip and strangely directs him to a most desolate place: the wilderness between Jerusalem and Gaza. There he comes upon of all people the chief treasure official to the queen of Ethiopia. He is traveling back to his homeland after his pilgrimage to Jerusalem.

The repentance and baptism of this man happens even more easily than for the Samaritans, for this man shows readiness by what he is reading (the prophecies of Isaiah) and willingness to embrace the central priorities of Jewish life. All Philip has to do in this instance is explain how the passage that he is reading relates to Jesus. The man is so eager to learn that he reads his Scripture as he bumps along the desert trail! When another "chance" event occurs—they run into water along the way—it is easy for the man to seek baptism. Afterwards, the official goes on his way to Ethiopia and Philip to Azotus (Ashdod, on the coast) and eventually to Caesarea, where Philip will settle down and reappear at the end of my "unfinished tale."

So, Theophilus, the Seven are not stuck in a rut as they do their practical service. Yes, they are "table-waiters" (for that is the root meaning of the word I used), but it is service for God himself. And God has ordered them as second-generation agents for advancing the Kingdom pioneered by first-generation leaders. They are the vital reinforcements for the scattered and persecuted Church.

Acts 8:26–40 **26** But an angel of the Lord said to Philip, "Rise and go toward the south to the road that goes down from Jerusalem to Gaza." This is a desert road. **27** And he rose and went. And behold, an Ethiopian, a eunuch, a minister of the Candace, queen of the Ethiopians, in charge of all her treasure, had come to Jerusalem to worship **28** and was returning; seated in his chariot, he was reading the prophet Isaiah. **29** And the Spirit said to Philip, "Go up and join this chariot." **30** So Philip ran to him, and heard him reading Isaiah the prophet, and asked, "Do you understand what you are reading?" **31** And he said, "How can I, unless some one guides me?" And he invited Philip to come up and sit with him. **32** Now the passage of the scripture which he was reading was this: "As a sheep led to the slaughter or a lamb before its shearer is dumb, so he opens not his mouth. **33** In his humiliation justice was denied him. Who can describe his generation? For his life is taken up from the earth." **34** And the eunuch said to Philip, "About whom, pray, does the prophet say this, about himself or about someone else?" **35** Then Philip opened his mouth, and beginning with this scripture he told him the good news of Jesus. **36** And as they went along the road they came to some water, and the eunuch said, "See, here is water! What is to prevent my being baptized?" **37 38** And he commanded the chariot to stop, and they both went down into the water, Philip and the eunuch, and he baptized him. **39** And when they came up out of the water, the Spirit of the Lord caught up Philip; and the eunuch saw him no more, and went on his way rejoicing. **40** But Philip was found at Azotus, and passing on he preached the gospel to all the towns till he came to Caesarea.

1. Identify and consider how "chance encounters" in my life have turned out to be fruitful. Have there been some chance encounters that have turned out the opposite?

2. Pray for divine appointments to bear fruit in my life. How available do I make myself for God to use me in such surprising ways?

3. How does this story more easily demonstrate the truth of Peter's prediction of "refreshment" (Acts 3:21) for those who are believers?

# Chapter 9

## Who Are You, Lord?

How do I begin to describe Saul, the man you know as Paul? Since I have traveled with him and spent many long hours at his side, I could tell you many things I have observed in the man. As fascinating as that would be, I would rather view him from the perspective of what his life represents in the progress of the Way. He was yet another significant force in fulfilling the words of Jesus to be "witnesses to the ends of the earth." In this respect, Paul was huge.

I begin with his conversion, for in it there is a lesson for everyone. For in this event the Kingdom of God is writ large and provocatively for everyone, friend and foe, to see. And Saul/Paul was nothing if not provocative, lightning rod that he was.

Actually, as I tentatively suggested earlier, the turning point came earlier than the drama of his actual conversion. Something deep within his conscience tingled as he had a hand in the lynching of Stephen. He knew that something was wrong when the mob noticed the angelic countenance and rarified message in the undoing of the martyr. *Yes, something was wrong.* Still, the crowd succumbed to what the Sanhedrin had schemed, though Saul seems to have been entranced deep within. His soul refused to let go of Stephen's heavenly vision and speech.

It was the spirit of Jesus that Saul witnessed in those last moments of Stephen's life. Jesus came to the perpetrators through Stephen, and Saul knew it. Now that same Jesus waited for a rendezvous with him again, this time at a propitious crossroads in Saul's life.

I must confess to you that I had no sympathy for Saul's puritanical sentiments. Like many other zealots dwelling in Jerusalem, he had moved to Jerusalem from abroad to find his roots in the covenant. And like them, he had picked up hyper-judgmental interpretations of the way of life given to Israel. It led him to take acerbic measures against those who deviated from "the true religion." And the followers of Jesus, mostly ignorant and oblivious Galileans that they were, goaded him into hostile reactions. Whatever spiritual awakening had occurred at the death of Stephen Saul now actively resisted. He took it upon himself to track down and punish the Jesus followers.

Jerusalem did not suffice for the scope of his crusade. By now he was aware that poisonous Jesus ideas had spread into the surrounding regions— you already heard what I had to say about Philip in Samaria, for example. Now some evidence for the Way was reported in Damascus, and he decided to go after them once he had secured the approval and logistical support of the Sanhedrin elites.

Let me pick up the story details here. Saul continued relentlessly on the trail of believers in Damascus, but Jesus intervened along the way for a last-ditch confrontation. Though Saul reports this encounter in different ways, I think I can glean the points important for us to understand. First, light flashes, and Paul ends up on the ground. Why does he fall to the ground? Saul recognizes something in this fierce light, something that he has seen it before, briefly, the angelic aura in Stephen's face as he stood before the mob in Jerusalem.

Was he on the ground because of his unworthiness? Was he hurled there by supernatural force? Paul never did fully clarify what happened either in teaching or conversation. I would say that a mysterious blend of core forces was at work in him, emanating both from Jesus in heaven and Saul on earth. What does Saul on the ground tell us about our fundamental choice to follow Jesus? Is our position before Jesus based on fear or fellowship? Is it a judgment of our utter unworthiness for our mortal puniness, or a surrender to our deepest desire to be known?

Then come the stark words: 'Saul! Why do you persecute me?' And Saul answers: 'Who are you, Lord?' In those few words, Saul/Paul shows recognition of whom he is grappling with. It is the "Lord." And yet *who* is Lord? For Saul, the dim light of his Pharisaic upbringing allowed an internal sketch; yet it was so vague that the current visitation of a glorious Jesus dwarfed his previous understanding. Paul always describes that moment as one that left him blind and dependent on speechless companions for help. Would we not all be speechless when we try to interpret how God interacts with created beings? And when fierce godly light comes to our mortal understanding, do we not also lose our ability for self-guidance? With Saul, though, the process was completed in a whirlwind of activity; with us it lasts a lifetime. Thus, Jesus identifies himself to Saul.

But notice how. The revelation is not limited to the individualized person known as Jesus, born of Mary, crucified under Pilate, dying, and now alive. No, he is more: he is invisibly in the ones Saul has targeted for punishment. An attack on them is an attack on him. In this insight, Saul begins to reckon with something that will animate his later writings and works. *All* those who follow Jesus are in fact held together by an internal gravity, the core of which is Jesus himself. The power at the center emanates outwardly to solidify over time all those who let themselves be drawn together. Jesus is at the center, and Jesus is at the periphery.

Paul rises from the ground helpless. A turning of the tables for this ringleader and born instigator! Public humiliation is thus heaped on undisclosed but undoubtedly private failures. This stunning blow to Saul's inner compass now requires prolonged soul-searching. No wonder he goes for the next three days without food and water. He had encountered Jesus, and yet Jesus would leave him a daze until he encountered Jesus once again among the ones he had come to persecute. In his own life, the lesson about the corporate nature of Jesus would be drawn poignantly. Jesus was the one he met on Damascus Way, and Jesus he would meet in the saints of Damascus.

One other irony of Saul's conversion. For the rest of his life, Saul/Paul would insist that he was a true Apostle because he had met the risen Jesus. Yet the face-to-face encounter left him blind and helpless without the help of those around him. His healing and baptism would only come through Ananias and fellow believers. Otherwise the scales still would have prevented Saul from becoming the Paul we know today. Thus his apostleship rested on both the individual and the corporate Jesus.

> Acts 9:3–9 **3** Now as he journeyed he approached Damascus, and suddenly a light from heaven flashed about him. **4** And he fell to the ground and heard a voice saying to him, "Saul, Saul, why do you persecute me?" **5** And he said, "Who are you, Lord?" And he said, "I am Jesus, whom you are persecuting; **6** but rise and enter the city, and you will be told what you are to do." **7** The men who were traveling with him stood speechless, hearing the voice but seeing no one. **8** Saul arose from the ground; and when his eyes were opened, he could see nothing; so they led him by the hand

and brought him into Damascus. **9** And for three days he was without sight, and neither ate nor drank.

1. Compare my conversion to Saul's. How would I describe my own conversion in terms of divine initiative and human receptiveness?

2. Did my conversion give any insight to the corporate nature of Jesus? How is my encounter with Jesus both individual and corporate?

3. How was I either oblivious to my own failures or consumed with unachievably high standards for a divine relationship?

## Makeover

And what happens to Saul after his extreme makeover? Saul waxes strong in his native boldness, convinced that he should press on his target audience exactly the opposite message he had earlier promoted. His new zeal leads him to a flurry of activities, as if to make up for the damage he has caused. His listeners both in Damascus and Jerusalem simply don't know what to make of his newfound faith. Years will go by before the Twelve will fully trust his testimony.

In fact, Saul's fiery personality sparks such controversy and conflict that the few daring souls that befriend Saul send him off quietly to his home city Tarsus for a kind of "cooling off" period, out of the public eye. It was a time of self-imposed refuge and reflection. It will take some 8–10 years before you will see him back on the scene, although I don't speak much about this phase of Saul's life in my account. Suffice it to say, Saul has to mature and rethink what he assumed about the Kingdom of God. The visions and revelations I have heard him speak about, the mysterious things that he says are unutterable and inscrutable, well, they happened during those years.

I would suspect that during this time he figured out many of his ideas about the Church. Saul's hometown and upbringing probably contributed a lot to his later perspective about the inclusiveness of the Kingdom of God. Even though Saul earlier submitted to the most stringent teachings about his religion, he also learned from the confluence of languages and cultures so evident in Tarsus. Did you know, Theophilus, that his home was only twenty-five miles away from the famed Cilician Gates, the pass that connects Asia to Mediterranean ports? So it was a cosmopolitan and colorful place where Saul grew up and then returned to for all those years.

Acts 9:22–30 **22** But Saul increased all the more in strength, and confounded the Jews who lived in Damascus by proving that Jesus was the Christ. **23** When many days had passed, the Jews plotted to kill him, **24** but their plot became known to Saul. They were watching the gates day and night, to kill him; **25** but his disciples took him by night and let him down over the wall, lowering him in a basket. **26** And when he had come to Jerusalem he attempted to join the disciples; and they were all afraid of him, for they did not believe that he was a disciple. **27** But Barnabas took him, and brought him to the apostles, and declared to them how on the road he had seen the Lord, who spoke to him, and how at Damascus he had preached boldly in the name of Jesus. **28** So he went in and out among them at Jerusalem, **29** preaching boldly in the name of the Lord. And he spoke and disputed against the Hellenists; but they were seeking to kill him. **30** And when the brethren knew it, they brought him down to Caesarea, and sent him off to Tarsus.

1. What kinds of training have I received to qualify me for a career path? Have I submitted to such a regime for my own spiritual development? Why or why not?

2. How does my faith reflect my own background and social milieu? Is it helpful? How ought it to be taken into account when I represent my faith?

## The Inspector

Meanwhile, there was Peter. He seemed to be the roving delegate of the Twelve, who both confirmed and certified what developments were occurring as the movement spread. Notice, Theophilus, that I call it the "Church," even though it is not located in a particular town or place. The Church represents a unity of groups, now scattered over disparate areas—for example, the aforementioned Judea and Samaria—but also across the hinterlands of Galilee, not otherwise detailed in my earlier report. You might call my recognition of this global reality, "catholic," or in Greek, *kata* ("across"), plus *holos* ("the whole")—for that is the phrase I used for the first time.

So Peter has a lot of ground to cover. (Fortunately, he is not the only one sent out by the Twelve for this business.) One area he goes is even more removed from Jerusalem: the coastlands and Romanized cities on the Mediterranean. While I suppose you could highlight Peter's mission by the miracles he worked there, really, this was not of the same scope of what happened with Philip in Samaria.

At least at first. Things would radically change after he had made the rounds. In fact, I don't have a clue about what Peter was hoping to accomplish by this visit to the Plain of Sharon. All I can say is that Peter now was in position for God to use him powerfully. It would be a chain of events that I will recount in my next entry. He came to Lydda at first, then he was summoned to Joppa on the coast, and finally he ended up in the area where Caesarea lies. Here in this new Roman port city, Peter would find himself in the middle of something divinely orchestrated that he had only vaguely glimpsed several weeks before. The gate where the Gentiles had previously begged entrance—like the beggar at Beautiful Gate—now swung open, for a previously unimaginable access to divine realities.

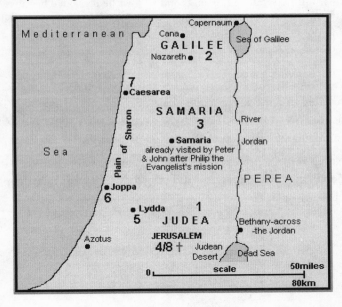

**Fig. 3: Peter's Missionary Travels.**
Used with permission: http://www.ccel.org/bible/phillips/JBPhillips.htm

Acts 9:32–43 **32** Now as Peter went here and there among them all, he came down also to the saints that lived at Lydda. **33** There he found a man named Aeneas, who had been bedridden for eight years and was paralyzed. **34** And Peter said to him, "Aeneas, Jesus Christ heals you; rise and make your bed." And immediately he rose. **35** And all the residents of Lydda and Sharon saw him, and they turned to the Lord. **36** Now there was at Joppa a disciple named Tabitha, which means Dorcas. She was full of good works and acts of charity. **37** In those days she fell sick and died; and when they had washed her, they laid her in an upper room. **38** Since Lydda was near Joppa, the disciples, hearing that Peter was there, sent two men to him entreating him, "Please come to us without delay." **39** So Peter rose and went with them. And when he had come, they took him to the upper room. All the widows stood beside him weeping, and showing tunics and other garments which Dorcas made while she was with them. **40** But Peter put them all outside and knelt down and prayed; then turning to the body he said, "Tabitha, rise." And she opened her eyes, and when she saw Peter she sat up. **41** And he gave her his hand and lifted her up. Then calling the saints and widows he presented her alive. **42** And it became known throughout all Joppa, and many believed in the Lord. **43** And he stayed in Joppa for many days with one Simon, a tanner.

1. Try to recall times when I felt I was involved in a chain of events that resulted in remarkable "coincidences?" Can I recall any other "coincidences" so far in Acts? (Hint: read again the story about Philip and the Ethiopian official in Acts 8.)

2. Name some representatives of the Church, either local or international, that I can recognize and pray for as they advance the progress of the Gospel.

# Chapter 10

## Another Pentecost

When I earlier described how Peter healed the lame man at the gate called Beautiful, I alluded to this event. If you remember, I said that the hour of the healing was important because it corresponded to the temple sacrifice called *Minhah*. In that moment, an intuitive flash came to Peter about how access once so exclusive to Jews now was available to others. Now the full extent of that insight played out in the chain of events that led Peter to Caesarea.

The mention of Caesarea should cause every halakic[1] Jew to wince. Why? Well, it was a port city through which streamed all the dangers for traditional execution of the ancestral way of life. Residing in the city were Romans and Greeks of every stripe along with apostate Jews and Samaritans. I suppose that every good Jew would think twice before exposing oneself to its noxious influences.

There was a Roman centurion who was stationed in Caesarea, whose name was Cornelius. Cornelius was famous for his sympathies and benefactions toward the institutions and accessories of the Jewish faith. He knew, for example, that every day the Jerusalem temple priest would duly offer intercessory sacrifice at the appointed hour; and so he and his household would observe their own solemn customs at that same time. Cornelius would pray toward Jerusalem, as any good Jew does, and he would intercede for himself, his family, and the world's redemption. In addition, he did his best to lead an exemplary life, cognizant of the one God who would hold him accountable for every deed.

1. "Halakah" represents the principles that guide daily life conduct for an observant Jew.

The day that Peter was visiting the Plain of Sharon, where Caesarea is located, Cornelius did his customary solemnities within his home. This time, however, something extraordinary happened. An angel appeared to him, assuring him that all his piety had arisen before God as a "memorial."

Now what is a "memorial," Theophilus? This is shorthand for the *Zik-karon*, the priestly prayer connected to the *Minhah* sacrifice of the ninth hour. In other words, the angel was recognizing Cornelius—a Roman war veteran in unsavory Caesarea—as a stand-in for a temple priest doing his duties. But even more extraordinary—think about it—heaven manifested itself on earth at the behest of this man, in a moment not far removed from what the Jews call *Shekinah*.[2] Theophilus, what priest would not long for such a visitation as the highest and purest goal of every temple prayer? In the Scriptures of the Jews, we have only a handful of privileged priests who drew so near a holy god and lived! (Again, Theophilus, I use my favorite word for this spiritual contemplation, ἀτενίζω [atenizō], that is, Cornelius had some kind of beatific access to the Almighty.) Cornelius, the Roman, has access to the Most High! Who else can make this claim for their prayers?

Peter, lodging nearby, goes to Cornelius when he is summoned. As he speaks to Cornelius and his assembled guests, guess what hour the event occurs? Yes, the same hour—the time of *Minhah*! This time however instead of a solitary messenger of God in response to a priestly service, now it is the corporate Jesus who manifests in the hearts of all those present before Peter. How can this be, for they all are Gentiles? Yet the amazement does not silence Peter's pronouncement that the Holy Spirit of Jesus is at work even among the despised Romans, Gentiles *par excellence*. It is, at it were, Pentecost again, but this time for the nations.

Three times, Theophilus, I reiterated what happened when I wrote you earlier. Why? Because I wanted to make sure that you know what it was that allows the Kingdom of God to include the Gentiles. This open door will increasingly be entered as we follow the steps of Saul, known as Paul, into this Gentile world.

> Acts 10:1–6 [1]At Caesarea there was a man named Cornelius, a centurion of what was known as the Italian Cohort, [2] a devout man who feared God with all his household, gave alms liberally to

---

2. Literally, the temporary "dwelling" or "settling" of the divine presence among the Israelites. The term is unattested in the Torah, but is a source of great speculation among the rabbis, who say it was the physical presence of God in the Ark of the Covenant in their Sinai wanderings and the climax of temple ritual.

the people, and prayed constantly to God. 3 About the ninth hour of the day he saw clearly in a vision an angel of God coming in and saying to him, "Cornelius." 4 And he stared at him in terror, and said, "What is it, Lord?" And he said to him, "Your prayers and your alms have ascended as a memorial before God. 5 And now send men to Joppa, and bring one Simon who is called Peter; 6 he is lodging with Simon, a tanner, whose house is by the seaside."

Acts 10:9–20 9 The next day, as they were on their journey and coming near the city, Peter went up on the housetop to pray, about the sixth hour. 10 And he became hungry and desired something to eat; but while they were preparing it, he fell into a trance 11 and saw the heaven opened, and something descending, like a great sheet, let down by four corners upon the earth. 12 In it were all kinds of animals and reptiles and birds of the air. 13 And there came a voice to him, "Rise, Peter; kill and eat." 14 But Peter said, "No, Lord; for I have never eaten anything that is common or unclean." 15 And the voice came to him again a second time, "What God has cleansed, you must not call common." 16 This happened three times, and the thing was taken up at once to heaven. 17 Now while Peter was inwardly perplexed as to what the vision which he had seen might mean, behold, the men that were sent by Cornelius, having made inquiry for Simon's house, stood before the gate 18 and called out to ask whether Simon who was called Peter was lodging there. 19 And while Peter was pondering the vision, the Spirit said to him, "Behold, three men are looking for you. 20 Rise and go down, and accompany them without hesitation; for I have sent them."

Acts 10:24–28 24 And on the following day they entered Caesarea. Cornelius was expecting them and had called together his kinsmen and close friends. 25 When Peter entered, Cornelius met him and fell down at his feet and worshiped him. 26 But Peter lifted him up, saying, "Stand up; I too am a man." 27 And as he talked with him, he went in and found many persons gathered; 28 and he said to them, "You yourselves know how unlawful it is for a Jew to associate with or to visit any one of another nation; but God has shown me that I should not call any man common or unclean."

Acts 10:34–35 34 And Peter opened his mouth and said: "Truly I perceive that God shows no partiality, 35 but in every nation any one who fears him and does what is right is acceptable to him."

Acts 10:44–48 **44** While Peter was still saying this, the Holy Spirit fell on all who heard the word. **45** And the believers from among the circumcised who came with Peter were amazed, because the gift of the Holy Spirit had been poured out even on the Gentiles. **46** For they heard them speaking in tongues and extolling God. Then Peter declared, **47** "Can any one forbid water for baptizing these people who have received the Holy Spirit just as we have?" **48** And he commanded them to be baptized in the name of Jesus Christ. Then they asked him to remain for some days.

1. Describe an incident where the Lord seemed to prepare the way for his will to unfold.

2. How does this story about Cornelius encourage me to prayerful intercession? What does it say about the dignity of personal and corporate prayer?

3. Reflect on the surprising things that the Holy Spirit has done in my life and among my connections. How should it make me refrain from pessimism about recurring problems? Does it give me hope? Pray that the Spirit works to bless again.

4. Summarize what Peter says to this first non-Jewish audience. Are there any parallels I can draw from this presentation of the Gospel story? Explain.

5. As I re-read this entire chapter, how much of the story is driven by divine initiative rather than human planning? How many other events of major consequence happen in the Book of Acts almost exclusively at divine initiative (e.g., Philip with the eunuch in Acts 8:26)?

# Chapter 11

## Transcript

The following official statement was passed on to me so that I could compile my book:

*Affidavit of the Jerusalem Council*

"Simon, whom we call Peter, reported to us his experiences, while travelling on the Plain of Sharon, and specifically his encounter with Gentiles in the port city of Caesarea. There he met with a centurion named Cornelius, whom many of us know to be a Roman official sympathetic to our beliefs and customs. Simon tells us that both he and Cornelius had corresponding prayer visions that drew them together into fellowship. While this mixing of Peter with Cornelius, a Gentile, is irregular and provocative in itself—and Peter testifies that he did so with deep concern—it was what happened in this meeting that constitutes the basis of this inquiry.

While Peter addressed Cornelius and his house, the Holy Spirit came upon them. Peter recognized that the whole constellation of events, culminating in this concrete divine intervention, led him to baptize them all in water. He personally gave us this interpretation of what happened: if John the Baptist recognized the Kingdom of God and baptized anyone who came to him, he (Peter) would do the same thing, for he had no other precedent for such an obvious divine visitation.

Needless to add, this was the second divine appointment with 'outsiders' to our group. Philip, one of the Seven, similarly said that he could not withhold baptism to the Ethiopian traveling back from Jerusalem—and now our Way has led to Africa.

However, this is an even larger proposition than another land, for it implies some kind of correspondence between Israelite and non-Israelite,

Jew and Gentile, before the Almighty. What is the nature of this relationship? Is it truly a sign of something truly radical unfolding in our days? Philip's case is an open door to a new place beyond our native land; yet Peter's actions involve us in a new paradigm, namely, mutuality between Jew and Gentile. All that we had once taken for granted now has to be reevaluated.

During the session, the Council's reaction was initially stark silence, shock at such a turn of events. Yet clearly it was a breath-taking pause to take stock of our spiritual heritage and interpretive traditions. Soon it was clear that awe replaced our reluctance and bewilderment. Yes, it is a holy fear upon which our resistance and doubt are presently subdued. Though we do not know where the Way is taking us, still our consensus that Peter's discernment was correct. A divine visitation is upon us with repercussions likely to unfold."

> Acts 11:15–18 **15** "As I began to speak, the Holy Spirit fell on them just as on us at the beginning. **16** And I remembered the word of the Lord, how he said, 'John baptized with water, but you shall be baptized with the Holy Spirit.' **17** If then God gave the same gift to them as he gave to us when we believed in the Lord Jesus Christ, who was I that I could withstand God?" **18** When they heard this they were silenced. And they glorified God, saying, "Then to the Gentiles also God has granted repentance unto life."

1. Have I ever been in a position where I can confirm or cancel fundamental directions a group or an organization is going? Give examples.

2. What modern or personal examples can I think of that parallels to what the Jerusalem Council is wrestling with here? Do I have a sense of what the divine counsel is for these parallels?

# Chapter 12

## Antioch

You need to remember the seed that was planted when Peter healed the crippled man outside the Temple compound at the gate called Beautiful. Peter realized something started at that moment, and he mulled over its implications. Perhaps it was the awe, the holy fear, that the Apostolic Council experienced as it discerned Peter's action in Caesarea. When he witnessed what happened with Cornelius, he knew that the seed had sprouted. It reminded him of the parable that Jesus had taught about how mustard seeds grow into bushes whose branches provide nesting places to flocks of birds.[1] Now our story turns to its full flowering.

Events were not long in coming. A city even further removed from Jerusalem and Caesarea was Antioch, the capital of the ancient Seleucid empire and commercial crossroads of Asia. Here some travelers themselves from Cyprus and Cyrene—familiar with the Way and street-wise with Gentiles—start to speak with Greeks about the implications of Peter's realization. And many of them responded and believed. This time though the Jerusalem Council does not send out its go-to delegates, Peter and John, but the trusted newcomer we met earlier, Barnabas. Remember him? He was the one who sold his property and handed it over to the Twelve. His integrity and radical commitment contrasted vividly with the duplicity of Ananias and Sapphira. He also discerned Saul's intentions when he first appeared in Jerusalem. Thus, he became the one the Council designated to check out what was going on in Antioch.

Mind you, the Council's choice in Barnabas shows two things: First, he represents the "new generation" of leadership. He is neither of the Twelve

---

1. Luke 13:18–21.

nor of the later Seven. Second, he still represents an apostolic responsibility for the growth of the Church, for it shows that development of the Way depends on Jerusalem's verdict. Thus, the Council stands as the center to confirm or deny what changes are claimed as inspired. You will notice Antioch's recognition of the Council's importance when it raised funds to send on to Jerusalem at a time when it too was financially strapped due to the famine. If nothing else, Antioch recognized the priority of Jerusalem in its commitments and duties.

Barnabas also is not slow to extend leadership to others. He remembers Saul after all these ten or so years, and goes to him in Tarsus. The rest of my account will show how brilliant this choice was for the extension of the Way into the wider world. The synergy of Saul's personality and Antioch's resources led to raising up and training a new corps of workers. All this dynamic growth was happening in the city of Antioch, so far from and so foreign to Jerusalem. Out of this swirling cauldron of various identities and ideas came a new nomenclature: "Christian" now labelled what would evolve from Antioch, and the name stuck for everyone in the Way.

> Acts 11:20–26 **20** But there were some of them, men of Cyprus and Cyrene, who on coming to Antioch spoke to the Greeks also, preaching the Lord Jesus. **21** And the hand of the Lord was with them, and a great number that believed turned to the Lord. **22** News of this came to the ears of the church in Jerusalem, and they sent Barnabas to Antioch. **23** When he came and saw the grace of God, he was glad; and he exhorted them all to remain faithful to the Lord with steadfast purpose; **24** for he was a good man, full of the Holy Spirit and of faith. And a large company was added to the Lord. **25** So Barnabas went to Tarsus to look for Saul; **26** and when he had found him, he brought him to Antioch. For a whole year they met with the church, and taught a large company of people; and in Antioch the disciples were for the first time called Christians.

> Acts 11:29–30 **29** And the disciples determined, every one according to his ability, to send relief to the brethren who lived in Judea; **30** and they did so, sending it to the elders by the hand of Barnabas and Saul.

1.  Have I ever been in the position of finding talent? Are there new faces or voices I need to recognize in projects I am involved in? What do I need to do to recognize and foster leadership?

2. How should I invest time for planning and training for the future? Find secular parallels to divine ways of "growing" the Church. How can I be a Barnabas to others?

3. What causes do I support? Why? Do I recognize a "Jerusalem" to my commitments or my group's allegiances? What personal contributions does my loyalty elicit from me?

## A Looking Glass World

The machinations of man often play out in the hidden workings of the Kingdom of God. No matter what role we play in the visible trappings of power—whether we think we are calling the shots or whether we feel powerless and pitiful, it is God who invisibly is at work to carry out his plans. Let me demonstrate this lesson in the fortunes of Herod surnamed Agrippa and Simon surnamed Peter.

- First, you might ask, Who is this Herod, who bears the family name so familiar to us from my previous story of Jesus? He is grandson of the great Herod who dominated the country of Palestine, thanks to his Roman connections. This Herod, though, was the boyhood friend of Augustus Caesar in Rome, and was invested with control of huge swaths of land in addition to Judea and Jerusalem.

- His privileged position with the Roman authorities allowed him to operate imperiously, executing one of the Twelve, James, brother of John and son of Zebedee. This act redressed an issue that went back to the earliest conflict between Jesus and the Judean Status Quo: Jesus and his band of upstarts threatened those who were in power. When those elites praised Herod's deed, he had no qualms about arresting another prominent member of the Twelve, Simon Peter. The stakes were higher here, as Simon Peter was the face of the Twelve in many of the stories I have already narrated to you.

- The Herods are consummate connivers, Theophilus: by carrying out these deeds during the days of Unleavened Bread, Herod Jr. both reminds the Judeans of Herod Sr.'s action taken against Jesus at that same time of year, and yet he cleverly cloaks his plots in pieties by delaying Peter's execution until after the holy season. To signal his resolute intention, Herod locks up Peter under round-the-clock surveillance, chaining him in place between two soldiers. Then he surrounds the prison cell with at least two layers of vigilant guards. There would be no Jesus-like deliverance for Peter!

So what can the Church do against such machinations? What can we do when the odds are so stacked against us, Theophilus? Our position seems so weak—it cannot defend itself against worldly powers. We have seen this time and time again in my many tales about the Twelve and the Seven facing imprisonment, interrogations, and outright executions. Not only this, but the Twelve—as I said, symbolizing how Jesus would reconstitute the twelve tribes of Israel—are increasingly fading away over time anyway. Yes, replacements come forward, but they too seem to be scattered. Herod killed James, has Peter in his hands to execute, and soon would eliminate all the Twelve, and likely thereafter hunt down all vestiges of Church leadership.

In the teeth of its apparent demise, urgent prayer is the Church's only recourse—as it is for us at this present time. What of Peter's perspective? He is oblivious to the divine designs for him at this low point of his life. As helpless as a toddler in den of jackals, he is yet the darling prize of sovereign search-and-rescue mission. As Peter tells the story, his actual state was lethargy and grogginess when God sent an angel to intervene. Is victory snatched from sure defeat except in fairy tales and dreams? The possibility of rescue was so far removed from our hero's consciousness that the angel had to remind him to put on his clothes! Chains fell off, the gate of iron opened up, and now he was free! Only then did Peter in his ineptitude realize he had been given freedom.

Then the story turns comical. For in Peter's realization that the forces of the Kingdom had secured his release through such things as iron chains and gates falling away before him, it is the door to Mary's house of true-blue intercessors that stays closed. How truly the gates of hell yield to the Church while the gates of the Church often stay closed to heavenly succor! For the servant girl Rhoda is so startled by Peter's appearance that she forgets to open up the door to him. We can smile at Peter's witlessness in jail and the disciples' skepticism in Mary's house, Theophilus, for so often it is the answer to our prayers that we write off to fantastical visions, naïve witnesses, and remote angels. We are as oblivious as they when God is at work in our midst.

For counterpoise, let us return to Herod Agrippa. Even though Peter and the Twelve had escaped the clutches of his plot, I am sure Herod felt that their reprieve was temporary. From his position of sovereignty, he could simply blame the setback on others and go on with life until the opportune moment arose again. Herod was at his prime, and everyone played up to his oversized ego.

In this case, the invisible working of the Kingdom turned on Herod. Peter knew from the get-go that miracles only accompanied him, and he urged others (like the godly Cornelius) not to put him on a pedestal for any special powers. Herod, on the other hand, took pleasure in godlike praise addressed to him. He had styled himself as the provider of food and benefits for his subjects, as if he were a divine cornucopia. And truly his land did provide trade and provision when the famine I spoke of earlier hit. The irony is that soon after an angel paid tribute to Peter by delivering him, another angel struck down Herod and smote him with worms. I hope you caught it: Peter is standing in angelic graces beyond credibility, while Herod is a carrier of worms, an image of hypocritical and bloated vanity.

I hope you enjoyed seeing the Kingdom from both angles, Herod's and Peter's. I signed off this dramatic story in my earlier account to you by saying that "the word of God grew and multiplied"—thus, the machinations of man are child's play in the hands of God. While we wring our hands in fear, we must remember that the One who sits in the heavens laughs. . . .

Acts 12:1–2 ¹About that time Herod the king laid violent hands upon some who belonged to the church. ² He killed James the brother of John with the sword; ³ and when he saw that it pleased the Jews, he proceeded to arrest Peter also. This was during the days of Unleavened Bread. ⁴ And when he had seized him, he put him in prison, and delivered him to four squads of soldiers to guard him, intending after the Passover to bring him out to the people. ⁵ So Peter was kept in prison; but earnest prayer for him was made to God by the church.

Acts 12:6–16 ⁶ The very night when Herod was about to bring him out, Peter was sleeping between two soldiers, bound with two chains, and sentries before the door were guarding the prison; ⁷ and behold, an angel of the Lord appeared, and a light shone in the cell; and he struck Peter on the side and woke him, saying, "Get up quickly." And the chains fell off his hands. ⁸ And the angel said to him, "Dress yourself and put on your sandals." And he did so. And he said to him, "Wrap your mantle around you and follow me." ⁹ And he went out and followed him; he did not know that what was done by the angel was real, but thought he was seeing a vision. ¹⁰ When they had passed the first and the second guard, they came to the iron gate leading into the city. It opened to them of its own accord, and they went out and passed on through one street; and immediately the angel left him. **11** And Peter came to himself, and said, "Now I am sure that the Lord has sent his angel and rescued me from the hand of Herod and from all that the Jewish people were expecting." **12** When he realized this, he went to the house of Mary, the mother of John whose other name was Mark, where many were gathered together and were praying. **13** And when he knocked at the door of the gateway, a maid named Rhoda came to answer. **14** Recognizing Peter's voice, in her joy she did not open the gate but ran in and told that Peter was standing at the gate. **15** They said to her, "You are mad." But she insisted that it was so. They said, "It is his angel!" **16** But Peter continued knocking; and when they opened, they saw him and were amazed.

Acts 12:21–24 **21** On an appointed day Herod put on his royal robes, took his seat upon the throne, and made an oration to them. **22** And the people shouted, "The voice of a god, and not of man!" **23** Immediately an angel of the Lord smote him, because he did not give God the glory; and he was eaten by worms and died. **24** But the word of God grew and multiplied.

1. Can I recall instances of "poetic justice" and reversals in my life? Describe them. Are there any in history?

2. What lessons can I learn from this story about prayer in the face of hopeless odds? How do God's answers to prayer often get dismissed or rejected as divinely ordained? Think of any prayers that have been answered in ways I was not expecting or in ways that only later showed them divinely ordained.

# Chapter 13

## Swirling Cauldron

If Barnabas and Saul represented a new generation of leaders, Antioch represented that place where there was a new beginning for the Way. Remember how "Christian" was coined as a word to describe this hybrid society of Jew and Greek in that far-away and foreign city. Remember how I said it was a "swirling cauldron" of various identities and ideas. Now consider the joining together of the types of individuals. Highly diverse and potent. You had there some gifted teachers, as you will soon find out when we talk about Saul. Then you had far-sighted prophets, a first in the Church outside of Jerusalem.

Prophets and teachers. Why this combination? Teaching gives the foundation for the group to understand its background and pedigree. Considering the motley composition of Antioch, the believers had to learn about the calling and history of Israel and about its institutions and offices, much as I am trying to familiarize you with, Theophilus. But prophecy is that lightning rod that makes it all come alive in the current circumstances. If the cauldron has many ingredients, prophecy is the seasoning that makes the concoction a specialty of the house (so to speak). Prophecy takes the teaching and gives it direction. In this case, it is prophecy that nudges folks into action and excitement. Prophetic ideas and plans must be based on a solid foundation laid by teachers. The two work hand in hand.

On top of this, you had the mixture of ethnic and social backgrounds among these prophets and teachers. Barnabas of course originally came from Cyprus and was highly regarded by the Jerusalem leaders. He recruited Saul to come from Tarsus after his ten years of retreat and study. Two came from Africa: Simeon the Black and Lucius from Cyrene—a man who could also do well with Latin-speakers from the western side of the Roman Empire. One grew up with the very Herod Antipas that I told you about a few chapters ago, and thus this "Manaen" hailed from distinguished origins going back to Palestine.

Who could tell how long this swirling cauldron could simmer things together without boiling over? There were so many combustible ingredients among this bunch that it is no wonder that eventually major direction for the Church would rise out of Antioch. Even short term, we would see its main instigators, Barnabas and Saul, disagree and part company when it came to mission. Yes, the ingredients were here for a potent brew of leaders!

The main thing that unfolded in these heady days was that the spirit of Jesus, so present from the Pentecost days in Jerusalem, communicated to the believers in Antioch. They had to "set apart" two of them for the "work to which I [the Holy Spirit] have called them." This implied a sense of separation from common routines and activities... so that they would free for divine use. This is the basis of what we call "holiness," a nurtured and spiritually combustible condition for which there is very little to compare in your Greco-Roman world.... Perhaps the Vestal Virgins of Rome comes to mind.

Anyway, two men were chosen and requisitioned, as if the Almighty claimed them as his possession. The two were Barnabas and Saul. Their mission: to be "sent off." To confirm this plan as the Lord's, all the others laid their hands on them to show solidarity and support. These two would no longer live a conventional life.

> Acts 13:1–4 ¹Now in the church at Antioch there were prophets and teachers, Barnabas, Simeon who was called Niger, Lucius of Cyrene, Manaen a member of the court of Herod the tetrarch, and Saul. ² While they were worshiping the Lord and fasting, the Holy Spirit said, "Set apart for me Barnabas and Saul for the work to which I have called them." ³ Then after fasting and praying they laid their hands on them and sent them off. ⁴ So, being sent out by the Holy Spirit, they went down to Seleucia; and from there they sailed to Cyprus.

1.  Is diversity an important component of human progress? Can I think of any enterprises that developed because of multicultural participation? Describe the dynamics involved.

2. Have I ever been a part of the "ground floor" of a big change or movement? Did I see elements of teaching and prophecy in this development? How so?

3. Are there people who are "set apart" by God today? How am I set apart in small ways? Have I ever felt "sent off" by the Lord for some mission? What was it like?

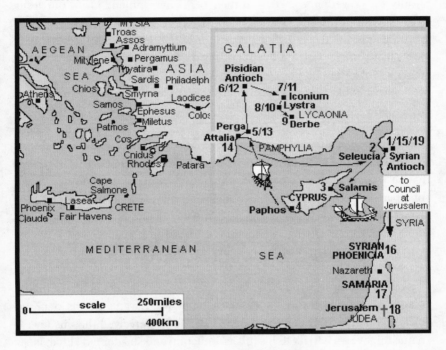

**Fig. 4: Paul's Missionary Journey with Barnabas.**
Used with permission: http://www.ccel.org/bible/phillips/JBPhillips.htm

## On the Road

Saul's zeal combined with his perceptiveness always has made him a unique individual, or maybe I should say a "force," for whatever team he is with. In this case, he was on the front end of the learning curve that the Spirit of Jesus was now precipitating in our circles, namely, that the Gentiles were objects of the divine plan. For Saul it was an all-consuming realization that hit him after he left Antioch and traveled abroad.

Let me try to walk through the essential steps that led Paul to make this major investment in reaching out to the Gentile people. First, in Cyprus Barnabas and Saul ran into a Jewish charlatan named Bar-Jesus, who combined the trickery of magic with enough of the divine truths given to Israel to sound credible. In other words, he as a Jew was the mirror reflection of Cornelius as a Gentile: someone searching the other side of supernatural reality for powers not present in their own environment. Only, Bar-Jesus was moving in the circles away from the truth and Cornelius toward the truth. Even Saul, the erstwhile persecutor of the Way, recognized that Bar-Jesus had gone far beyond the boundary of ignorance and was becoming a willing tool of falsehood.

What cooks the goose also cooks the gander: Saul called down blindness upon his Jewish adversary in the same way that he once had been temporarily blinded by the light of the risen Jesus. Paul instantly recognized that what should have been the straight path of Israel for all to follow through the testimony of this transplanted Jew (Bar-Jesus) now was as crooked as to double back on itself. Paul's/Saul's action took the form of a performative prophecy, much like you might read in the Scriptures of Israel, only in the vein of a curse instead of an obvious blessing. How useful curses are for advancing the Kingdom instead of blessing I will leave for you to contemplate, Theophilus—they are in our spiritual repertoire, but rarely invoked.

This display of symbolism dazzled Bar-Jesus's former client, the highly placed proconsul for the island, whose name was Sergius Paulus. Saul did pick up one tip from Bar-Jesus: just as Bar-Jesus perceived that his Jewish name might be a barrier to his full assimilation and so adopted "Elymas" as his calling card, so Saul became "Paul" to almost all of his connections in the Gentile world.

This was step one in the process of redirecting the attention of both Barnabas and (now) Paul toward the Gentiles. And at this point, they journey back to the mainland, Asia Minor, and start their overland tour. In all of the cities they visit, they first look for Jewish confreres. They naturally know the protocols and customs for making these connections with their diaspora community. Among the chief habits is a regular observance of Saturday as a day of recollection, gathering, and community prayer—a service called "Shabbat," held in a place called a synagogue. When it comes time for discourse on the prearranged reading of the day, well, that is when Paul and Barnabas would make their appeal to the assembled community members.

I won't get into the details of Paul's inaugural speech, but it is geared for an audience that knows the ebb and flow of Israel's temperamental relationship with the Most High. Some of the high points you by now would recognize, but you would have to be well attuned to Jewish issues to pick up on everything both current and past to put it altogether. Needless to say, Paul's persuasiveness also figured in, and many of the townspeople in attendance turned around in their thinking. Now Paul and Barnabas came sharply into focus, and the disciples did not waste this fifteen minutes of fame.

Alas, where grace abounds, sin does also: The resident Jews objected to what Paul said. Perhaps they resented the suggestion that their leaders in Jerusalem were in some way to blame for the death of Jesus. Perhaps they were jealous that Paul would so eloquently defend poor and ignorant Galileans instead of the more educated and genteel Judeans that they themselves represented. Or maybe it was simply that he had the hubris to apply weighty biblical judgments to his own Jewish forbears—and by extension to present Jewish company. Who can say what propels rumors and gossip?

However, when the next Shabbat came around, these opponents were as much in force vocally against Paul and Barnabas as the curious crowd was in number. It then dawned on the Apostles that this was what the Spirit had been indicating, namely, that their mission to advance the light of Israel would be for the Gentiles. It was a much bigger step than any of their predecessors had ever taken, for they would soon become immersed in the Gentile world and not simply running into them in the margins. Where this path would lead, neither Paul nor Barnabas knew; yet that it was divinely ordained and their mission Paul spent the rest of his life defending.

I have often alluded, Theophilus, that divine sovereignty so outstrips human plans that one can imagine guffaws from heaven. Case in point: Barnabas and Paul had not set out with a worldwide mission to the Gentiles in mind. Yet it was through these human agents, committed to a work beyond their scope, that the Kingdom advanced. And the disciples intuited its reality in spite of all the affliction they would encounter along the Way.

This awareness filled them with joy because they were walking in the same paths as those who followed Jesus from the first. He told that generation what to do and warned them not to worry about what others would do against them. Instead, just let go of the conflicts arising from those who opposed them, and "shake the dust from their feet."

What did Jesus mean by this odd expression? Jesus said this action would serve "as a testimony against them." If the listeners had accepted the Kingdom that the disciples of Jesus announced, the messengers would have no need to shake the dust. They would share the same ground with their audience, and they would share responsibility for what transpired as they went about the people who received their message. But if they shook off the dust, that meant a complete separation. The disciples were then free to move on without taking responsibility for what happened to the audience. They could keep going without guilt, care, or even bitterness to the next junction.

Anyway, Barnabas and Paul left this first location on the mainland called Psidian Antioch filled with joy and the Holy Spirit. Why so much fervor, you ask? Recall that when the Twelve were persecuted publicly and endured "dishonor for the sake of the name," they too were filled with joy. It is the public association of the disciples with Jesus that brings them into his identity and fate. Such a status both thrills and sobers. On one hand, the Spirit gave them witness on Pentecost that they were united with Jesus; on the other hand, the world surrounding them had its own way of confirming this status by persecuting and expelling them. It was true of Jesus, true for the Twelve, and now true for Paul and Barnabas. Theophilus, remember that when there are forces that target you because of your public witness to Jesus, you are now a target for the special care of the Holy Spirit, for God sees you—together with Paul, Barnabas, and the Twelve—as associated with his Son. Paul had learned the lesson of a corporate Jesus on his way to Damascus.

> Acts 13:3–4 **3** Then after fasting and praying they laid their hands on them and sent them off. **4** So, being sent out by the Holy Spirit, they went down to Seleucia; and from there they sailed to Cyprus.

> Acts 13:6–11 **6** When they had gone through the whole island as far as Paphos, they came upon a certain magician, a Jewish false prophet, named Barjesus. **7** He was with the proconsul, Sergius Paulus, a man of intelligence, who summoned Barnabas and Saul and sought to hear the word of God. **8** But Elymas the magician (for that is the meaning of his name) withstood them, seeking to turn away the proconsul from the faith. **9** But Saul, who is also called Paul, filled with the Holy Spirit, looked intently at him **10** and said, "You son of the devil, you enemy of all righteousness, full of all deceit and villainy, will you not stop making crooked the

straight paths of the Lord? **11** And now, behold, the hand of the Lord is upon you, and you shall be blind and unable to see the sun for a time." Immediately mist and darkness fell upon him and he went about seeking people to lead him by the hand.

Acts 13:14–16 **14**And on the sabbath day they went into the synagogue and sat down. **15** After the reading of the law and the prophets, the rulers of the synagogue sent to them, saying, "Brethren, if you have any word of exhortation for the people, say it." **16** So Paul stood up, and motioning with his hand said: "Men of Israel, and you that fear God, listen."

Acts 13:24–25 **24** Before his coming John had preached a baptism of repentance to all the people of Israel. **25** And as John was finishing his course, he said, 'What do you suppose that I am? I am not he. No, but after me one is coming, the sandals of whose feet I am not worthy to untie.'

Acts 13:26–35 **26** "Brethren, sons of the family of Abraham, and those among you that fear God, to us has been sent the message of this salvation. **27** For those who live in Jerusalem and their rulers, because they did not recognize him nor understand the utterances of the prophets which are read every sabbath, fulfilled these by condemning him. **28** Though they could charge him with nothing deserving death, yet they asked Pilate to have him killed. **29** And when they had fulfilled all that was written of him, they took him down from the tree, and laid him in a tomb. **30** But God raised him from the dead; **31** and for many days he appeared to those who came up with him from Galilee to Jerusalem, who are now his witnesses to the people. **32** And we bring you the good news that what God promised to the fathers, **33** this he has fulfilled to us their children by raising Jesus; as also it is written in the second psalm, 'Thou art my Son, today I have begotten thee.' **34** And as for the fact that he raised him from the dead, no more to return to corruption, he spoke in this way, 'I will give you the holy and sure blessings of David.' **35** Therefore he says also in another psalm, 'Thou wilt not let thy Holy One see corruption.'

Acts 13:40–43 **40** Beware, therefore, lest there come upon you what is said in the prophets: **41** 'Behold, you scoffers, and wonder, and perish; for I do a deed in your days, a deed you will never believe, if one declares it to you.'" **42** As they went out, the people begged that these things might be told them the next sabbath. [43] And when the meeting of the synagogue broke up, many Jews and devout converts to Judaism followed Paul and Barnabas, who spoke to them and urged them to continue in the grace of God.

Acts 13:44–45 [44] The next sabbath almost the whole city gathered together to hear the word of God. [45] But when the Jews saw the multitudes, they were filled with jealousy, and contradicted what was spoken by Paul, and reviled him.

Acts 13:48–52 [48] And when the Gentiles heard this, they were glad and glorified the word of God; and as many as were ordained to eternal life believed. [49] And the word of the Lord spread throughout all the region. [50] But the Jews incited the devout women of high standing and the leading men of the city, and stirred up persecution against Paul and Barnabas, and drove them out of their district. [51] But they shook off the dust from their feet against them, and went to Iconium. [52] And the disciples were filled with joy and with the Holy Spirit.

1. Have I ever stumbled on a completely new thing that changes my perspective for doing things? Give an example. Can I think of anything like it that parallels the spiritual world?

2. Think of movements or ideas that combine enough truth with falsehood to sell? Are there things in my life which are "mixed" (in motivation or in authority) enough to communicate the wrong thing to others? How can I free myself from "mixed" agendas?

3. Consider the difference between a curse and a blessing. How do what seem to be bad things sometimes make a positive impact on problems? Have I ever resorted to what Saul seems to carry out on Bar-Jesus?

# Chapter 14

## Afflictions: Iconium

If you thought this last escapade would be the finale for their mission to Asia Minor, you would be quite mistaken about anything involving Paul. Paul was not a quitter, and he had no space for anyone who gave up. Instead he and Barnabas pressed further into the province of Asia Minor, first to Iconium and then even further to Lystra and Derbe. Mind you, Theophilus, these were quite isolated and alien areas for them. What do I mean? Well, to begin with they would walk from place to place, sometimes scores of miles along roads that were physically tortuous and humanly treacherous.

Even more disorienting was the fact that there would be fewer and fewer people who would be fluent in their language or plug into the customs and lifestyles that you and I would know from our civilized perspectives. And finally, most people they encounter as they penetrate Asia Minor's interior would have almost no knowledge of their basic premises about faith in the one God who established a worldwide kingdom through Israel's messiah.

Their habit was first to find kindred souls—Jewish ex-pats—and barring this, to reach out to anyone who would listen. The green light to Gentiles did not rule out continuing their assumptions that fellow Jews would understand more easily the testimony that they bore concerning the Kingdom of God.

The first destination, some eighty-five miles away, was Iconium. They attracted much interest from the general public at first, and I mean from both Jew and Gentile. As time went on, some Jews stirred up nagging controversy around them, but they remained in Iconium in spite of it all, witnessing and organizing those in sympathy with their message. It was

75

only when they learned that the opposition had hardened into a full-bore conspiracy that Paul and Barnabas read the handwriting on the wall and moved on another twenty miles down the road to Lystra.

> Acts 14:1–3 ¹Now at Iconium they entered together into the Jewish synagogue, and so spoke that a great company believed, both of Jews and of Greeks. ² But the unbelieving Jews stirred up the Gentiles and poisoned their minds against the brethren. ³ So they remained for a long time, speaking boldly for the Lord, who bore witness to the word of his grace, granting signs and wonders to be done by their hands.

## Afflictions: Lystra, Part I

Lystra was another place altogether. Here there were no synagogues to begin with, so far from the beaten path was this city for Jewish sojourners. Plus, there was virtually no way to reach the crowds because so few spoke Greek, the language that Paul and Barnabas used to communicate. That meant that the two had to resort to more blunt ways of announcing the Kingdom: miracles and wonders. Paul, like Peter, always seems to have a sixth sense focused on the supernatural, and just like Peter gazed at that hopelessly crippled man at the gate called Beautiful, so Paul suddenly was transfixed (think ἀτενίζω [atenizō]) by another cripple whom no one in Lystra had ever seen walk. And just like Peter's healing, this man not only walked but leaped up into the spotlight of everyone's attention.

> Acts 14:8–10 ⁸ Now at Lystra there was a man sitting, who could not use his feet; he was a cripple from birth, who had never walked. ⁹ He listened to Paul speaking; and Paul, looking intently at him and seeing that he had faith to be made well, ¹⁰ said in a loud voice, "Stand upright on your feet." And he sprang up and walked.

## Afflictions: Lystra, Part II

All of a sudden, everyone knew that these strangers from afar represented something that was totally outside the boundaries of the natural world. The only thing they knew from their own upbringing was the fantasy and folklore of Zeus and Hermes. And now Paul had to negotiate between the worlds of Asia Minor's mythology and the Bible's Kingdom of God. How do you do so when the audience does not know even the basics of the language you speak? The crowd could pick up through the ensuing gestures that Paul and Barnabas were unhappy with the Lystrans' assessment of the miracle. And they struggled to understand Paul's Greek words related to a unique and all-powerful god who made and transcended the world and its forces. How remote were Paul and Barnabas's explanations from the visible and visceral realities they met every day in the form of fickle health, capricious weather, and excessive sexuality.

> Acts 14:15–17 **15** "Men, why are you doing this? We also are men, of like nature with you, and bring you good news, that you should turn from these vain things to a living God who made the heaven and the earth and the sea and all that is in them. **16** In past generations he allowed all the nations to walk in their own ways; **17** yet he did not leave himself without witness, for he did good and gave you from heaven rains and fruitful seasons, satisfying your hearts with food and gladness."

1. What are the ways I would argue for my beliefs without insisting on reading the Bible? How can I appeal to natural reason or revelation to communicate this message?

2. Am I convinced of these basic truths that Paul alludes to in this passage? Go through each attribute that Paul ascribes to God and ask whether each is true for you.

## Afflictions: Lystra, Part III

It was in the midst of this melee that Paul and Barnabas's dogged opponents from Iconium caught up with them. They knew the native language called Lycaonian since they occasionally had dealings with Lystrans, and so the spin control was now in their hands. They soon turned the crowd's favorable stir into an ugly stampede against the strangers.

Paul, the one they identified with Hermes, they attacked and stoned. I suppose they knew that Hermes has the reputation for playing tricks and duping people of their valuables. The Iconian conspirators had apparently convinced the citizens of Lystra that Paul deserved a good thrashing to the point of death. They dragged him out of town, probably depositing him in the paupers' graveyard to the care of his ilk. And there amongst his sympathizers, surprisingly, he rose up! Not only that, but he returned to the city!

Didn't I tell you that Paul doesn't quit, even when it comes to the reins of physical life?

Lystra in uproar, they move on another sizable distance to Derbe, a place I will speak about later. Suffice it here to say that it was the endpoint of their journey into Asia Minor for the time being. Rather than take the lumps of their labor and be the wiser for it by going directly to the base city where they began it all—Antioch in Seleucia—amazingly they retrace their tortuous steps and visit the remnant groups they left behind. Their message now to each destination: "Through many tribulations we must enter the Kingdom of God." The willingness to go back this harrowing way only confirmed that they were resolutely sure that it was the Spirit who set them apart and led them out in the first place. We will follow Paul in the stories ahead, because I am sure it was his steeled inner resolution that will illustrate this message to continue despite all the setbacks and personal attacks.

> Acts 14:19–22 **19** But Jews came there from Antioch and Iconium; and having persuaded the people, they stoned Paul and dragged him out of the city, supposing that he was dead. **20** But when the disciples gathered about him, he rose up and entered the city; and on the next day he went on with Barnabas to Derbe. **21** When they had preached the gospel to that city and had made many disciples, they returned to Lystra and to Iconium and to Antioch, **22** strengthening the souls of the disciples, exhorting them to continue in the faith, and saying that through many tribulations we must enter the kingdom of God. **23** And when they had appointed elders for them in every church, with prayer and fasting they committed them to the Lord in whom they believed.

1. Go back through the last two chapters and make a list of all the hardships Paul and Barnabas endured. If I were Paul, would I have returned to the places mentioned after my experiences? Explain why or why not.

2. Can I think of any tribulations visited on me while I have struggled to make progress on life's priorities? Describe them.

3. Do I have a support group, like Paul, who can encircle me when it seems like I am ready to fail? Who would be on the team? How do they support me?

CHAPTER 14

# Afflictions: Conclusion

Paul and Barnabas do not look at the dark side of their mission into Antioch, Lystra, Iconium, and Derbe. Instead they see the whole venture as the Kingdom of God advancing. What has the Almighty done here? For Paul and the future of the Church, this project was extremely beneficial. It was not a series of setbacks and last stands because of the forces arrayed against them. Rather it was a huge perspective change that brought in the Gentiles: an "open door" through which they must now proceed. An "open door" only for those who know how heaven laughs . . .

> Acts 14:27 And when they arrived, they gathered the church together and declared all that God had done with them, and how he had opened a door of faith to the Gentiles.

1. Do I have an accountability team, like Paul and Barnabas had from their sponsors in Antioch? Who would be my sponsors, or someone I report to? How do they guide and help me?

2. Identify some project or program that you began or are helping. First, go over the challenges involved. Second, ask God to show you how doors are open because of what happened. Third, be prepared to tell "the church" what God has done because this extra effort your program demanded.

# Chapter 15

## Pillar and Bulwark of Truth

Attention now boomerangs back to Jerusalem, as we realize that the whole forward thrust of Paul and Barnabas into the Gentile world is still connected to Israel and its salvation history. As brilliant a mission as has begun, it cannot fix itself as an autonomous and eternal reality with supernatural leverage "against which the forces of hell will not prevail" (to cite the words of Jesus). All along I have hoped to impart in you, Theophilus, a sense that you are part of something much bigger than your lifetime and your birthplace.

No matter one's ideals and talents and powers, no one can stand alone. And this goes for the Church: it is joined together over time and place by something outside itself. Saul/Paul crashed into it when he pursued scattered believers as far away as Damascus, and he learned that it was Jesus himself whom he persecuted, for he holds different pieces together from widespread places. What holds for physical space and individuals also holds for levels of responsibility and decision-making within social organizations. From Saul's conversion story on Damascus road, you learned about the Spirit of Jesus who works sovereignly and directly on individuals; from the story of Barnabas and Saul, the lesson is that the connection also comes from the Church itself in its processes and structures, something you can compare to how civic institutions form identity within the city-state. So even when there is honest division in the body politic and disagreement among individuals, it need not threaten the fundamental progress and solidarity of the Church.

The context is that Paul and Barnabas's mission to Asia Minor came to the attention of delegates visiting from Judea. In the process of their touring and teaching, they heard about Paul and Barnabas's mission to Asia Minor.

When they complained that the inclusion of the Gentiles could not happen without making them Jews, it caused no small ruckus in the group.

Paul and Barnabas then led a team to Jerusalem to get a ruling from the Apostolic Council on the question. Even they saw the need for higher "official" approval for this new expansion. When they arrived they met with a similar division of opinion, with the more rigorous party of the Pharisees lobbying for the Gentiles to convert.

Two voices prevailed, and they both represented the most venerable elements of the Jerusalem Church: Peter and James. Peter's own experience came in his encounter with Cornelius and his household, something that everyone affirmed at that time even though they did not have a clue about how to incorporate Gentiles into the Church. James viewed Paul and Barnabas's mission as consistent with Peter's, and then he cited Scripture as a confirmation for including the Gentiles. Their stentorian opinions won the day for Paul and Barnabas.

While it might seem that this decision would be enough to take back to Antioch, something unparalleled happened for the Church: the writing down of the Council's decision for distribution and reading throughout all the Gentile areas. Why? This decision, James felt, needed even more than the Scriptures of Israel and a vote of the Council to hold its weight.

This recognition points to some facts that might have slipped by us, so let us pause for a moment. For one thing, the old guard is fading away. That is, the earliest eye-witnesses to Jesus and his Kingdom are disappearing, and a new generation—the Seven, the Council (Apostles *and* "elders") and its legates like Barnabas—need an anchor clinging fiercely to the foundation established in the early days.

So yes, it was a common decision of the Council, based on the senior opinions and certainly the Scriptures. But notice, Theophilus, they also packaged it as a document credited preeminently to the Holy Spirit. And it is meant to be official Church policy to be read in every city along with writings of Moses. Now that is a high claim to authority: inspiration and accreditation all at once!

Why would the Apostolic Council want this decree written down? For the same reason that I wrote my earlier accounts on Jesus and the Church. The written testimony serves as an anchor, even if the ship's sails are yanked to and fro by winds. For the Apostolic Council, its decision came from the earliest and most authoritative sources (Peter, James, the Scriptures). Yet from another perspective, look what else is going on: the earliest and most authoritative sources are fading away. On such an important topic, we have here only two of the Twelve on the scene to speak. On the mountain of Jesus's ascent, it was "the Twelve;" but now it is the Council—composed not as the Twelve, but as apostles *and* elders. And who delivers this message to Antioch? Primarily I point to two leaders, and neither is from the earliest witnesses: Judas and Silas, neither of whom have we heard from before. Yes, this is a new age that calls for a firm anchor.

Let me give you another illustration of this same idea: Barnabas came from Cyprus and served as the apostolic link for Saul in Jerusalem and Antioch, and so he is an intermediary for that phase of the Kingdom expanding into Antioch. But now the expansion has progressed beyond Antioch into a full mission to Gentiles, and Barnabas is insufficient and so will fade away in my story. Silas, the newcomer I mentioned above, will take his place; he is a bit more removed from the earliest foundation than Barnabas. When the mortality of human beings fails, it is time (so I maintain) for the institutional side to show its strong suit. Thus, we have the need, Theophilus, to write down our testimony as the Holy Spirit leads us. It is time for Scripture to rivet us together, and the "Apostolic Decree" is our model—and in my own modest way, I offer this writing before you.

> Acts 15:22–32 **22** Then it seemed good to the apostles and the elders, with the whole church, to choose men from among them and send them to Antioch with Paul and Barnabas. They sent Judas called Barsabbas, and Silas, leading men among the brethren, **23** with the following letter: "The brethren, both the apostles and the elders, to the brethren who are of the Gentiles in Antioch and Syria and Cilicia, greeting. **24** Since we have heard that some persons from us have troubled you with words, unsettling your minds, although we gave them no instructions, **25** it has seemed good to us, having come to one accord, to choose men and send them to you with our beloved Barnabas and Paul, **26** men who have risked their lives for the sake of our Lord Jesus Christ. **27** We have therefore sent Judas and Silas, who themselves will tell you the same things by word of mouth. **28** For it has seemed good to the Holy Spirit and to us to lay upon you no greater burden than these necessary things: **29** that you abstain from what has been sacrificed to idols and from blood and from what is strangled and from unchastity. If you keep yourselves from these, you will do well. Farewell." **30** So when they were sent off, they went down to Antioch; and having gathered the congregation together, they delivered the letter. **31** And when they read it, they rejoiced at

the exhortation. **32** And Judas and Silas, who were themselves prophets, exhorted the brethren with many words and strengthened them.

1. What are some of the advantages that an institution has over individual efforts? What are the problems an institution carries? How do I respect institutions in the organizations I am part of?

2. What are some of the institutions within the church I am part of? How do I show respect for them?

3. Does this view of "canonization" of Scripture fit how I think about the Bible? What seems to motivate the Jerusalem Church above to write down its decision? What seems to be the motivation of their endorsement of Paul and Barnabas (not mentioned above)? That is, how do Paul and Barnabas represent what they see as true signs of spiritual validity?

## Transformation

With the Council's recognition that recently added Gentiles had standing alongside of Jews, the riddle that had been with us almost from Day One began to disclose its scope. The geographic span of the Kingdom was now shown to outstrip Judea and Samaria, expanding into contiguous areas like Syria and the Lebanon, and even ricocheting into far-flung lands like Ethiopia and now Asia Minor. Its ethnic scope now stretched toward worldwide tether, with Jew and Gentile incorporated and all manner of language and culture in our assemblies. What was once a matter of Judea and Jerusalem temple and inherited Scriptures now burst into new categories of holy land and holy space and holy decisions.

To hold things together, Church leadership had both to hold on to past experiences and to recruit for future directions. I have in mind, Theophilus, three stalwarts who illustrate how the Church responded to that dynamic moment: Paul, Barnabas, and Silas. Paul represents the new force as a pioneer among the Gentiles, while Barnabas and Silas represent older ties to the Twelve and the Council. Barnabas served as bridge-builder, who first reached out to Paul and then traveled with him in the first missionary voyage. Silas was otherwise unknown, but came down to give the approval of the Apostles and the elders to the venture among the Gentiles.

Another dimension was that two younger recruits appear reflecting different reactions to Paul: on one hand, there is John Mark who abandoned Paul in Pamphylia; and on the other hand, there is Timothy, soon to join the mission, who is gung-ho to identify with Paul and even willing to have himself circumcised.

From this point on, the story will focus on Paul, not on Barnabas. Similarly, in this new generation of Church expansion, Timothy will play a major role in the development of the early Church, and Mark will vanish. Barnabas goes another—maybe safer?—direction and takes along the representative of past events (Mark), one who specifically had abandoned what Barnabas and Paul had begun in the mission.

Paul will take Silas, whom we know served earlier as courier for the Apostolic Decree "scripture" and had prophesied and encouraged in Antioch when he arrived there. Thus, Silas in himself is a wonderful portent of old and new: the Decree and prophecy.

To their company Paul will add another fresh face, Timothy, perhaps taking a chance but also relying on the general reputation of the young man. Paul himself is a quizzical hybrid of the cutting edge and the conventional: he baptizes Gentiles, but he is so adamant that Timothy be solidly Jewish that he circumcises Timothy himself! And he faithfully continues the link to the Church in Jerusalem (the past) by spreading to everyone the word of the Apostles and elders and utilizing their own representative Silas.

Who is right, Paul or Barnabas? You will see that the rest of my text will pull for Paul, whom it follows with singular focus. More immediately to the context, the final line I wrote below suggests that Paul and Company is responsible for the increase of the Church—and my silence about Barnabas and Company should speak loudly to you about my opinion. Though the word "increased" speaks to the Greek meaning of ἐπερίσσευον (*eperisseuon*) it masks the real implication that this new effort "abounded" or "enriched" everyone.

> Acts 15:35—16:5 **35** But Paul and Barnabas remained in Antioch, teaching and preaching the word of the Lord, with many others also. **36** And after some days Paul said to Barnabas, "Come, let us return and visit the brethren in every city where we proclaimed the word of the Lord, and see how they are." **37** And Barnabas wanted to take with them John called Mark. **38** But Paul thought best not to take with them one who had withdrawn from them in Pamphylia, and had not gone with them to the work. **39** And there arose a sharp contention, so that they separated from each other;

Barnabas took Mark with him and sailed away to Cyprus, **40** but Paul chose Silas and departed, being commended by the brethren to the grace of the Lord. **41** And he went through Syria and Cilicia, strengthening the churches. [Acts 16:1] And he came also to Derbe and to Lystra. A disciple was there, named Timothy, the son of a Jewish woman who was a believer; but his father was a Greek. **2** He was well spoken of by the brethren at Lystra and Iconium. **3** Paul wanted Timothy to accompany him; and he took him and circumcised him because of the Jews that were in those places, for they all knew that his father was a Greek. **4** As they went on their way through the cities, they delivered to them for observance the decisions which had been reached by the apostles and elders who were at Jerusalem. **5** So the churches were strengthened in the faith, and they increased in numbers daily.

1. Have I ever had to go separate ways from someone that I worked closely with? What were the signs and supports that helped me to navigate through troubled waters? Does God sometimes use honest disagreement to advance his work? Can I think of any personal examples?

2. Look back on some difficult decision and try to piece together how God figured into the process. Give thanks for his help or make amends for failures.

3. How do I prepare for future challenges? Am I involved in recruitment or training? How do I contribute for the Church's future in recruitment or training?

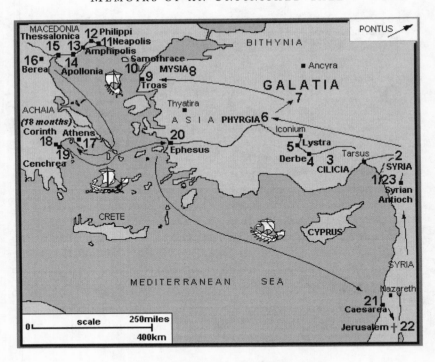

**Fig. 5: Paul's Missionary Voyage with Silas.**
Used with permission: http://www.ccel.org/bible/phillips/JBPhillips.htm

# Chapter 16

## Commentary

In the following section, I will put my original words first and then offer my interpretation on its meaning following. I figure this approach allows you to follow along more closely—as if you are traveling with us as strangers in a strange land.

> Acts 16:5–10 **5** So the churches were strengthened in the faith, and they increased in numbers daily. **6** And they went through the region of Phrygia and Galatia, having been forbidden by the Holy Spirit to speak the word in Asia. **7** And when they had come opposite Mysia, they attempted to go into Bithynia, but the Spirit of Jesus did not allow them; **8** so, passing by Mysia, they went down to Troas. **9** And a vision appeared to Paul in the night: a man of Macedonia was standing beseeching him and saying, "Come over to Macedonia and help us." **10** And when he had seen the vision, immediately we sought to go on into Macedonia, concluding that God had called us to preach the gospel to them.

## Change of Plans

What begins as an ordinary checkup on the mission field ends up as a whole new project with a whole different team of missionary workers. The ordinary trip would have involved Paul and Barnabas going by ship to Pisidian Antioch, Lystra, Iconium, and Derbe. Instead, Paul and Barnabas split over John Mark's involvement, with Barnabas going with John Mark by ship to Cyprus, and Paul going with Silas overland through Syria and Cilicia to their mission destinations. Paul apparently has the approval of the church in Antioch ("commended by the brethren to the grace of the Lord"), and he proceeds to build up the churches he had founded.

While he is in the backwoods area of Lycaonia—the same place where he was earlier called Hermes by the local rustics—he decides to install another team member, Timothy. Timothy is a perfect contributor to the team, for he is the son of a Greek father and a Jewish mother and knows the Scriptures well.[1] In time, Timothy would be raised up as Paul's right-hand man for establishing the churches—but that story is not mine to tell.

Now the three of them try to push the expansion ahead and meet only with failure and unfulfilled plans. My text says that they cannot even speak the word in the areas that they choose outside the Lycaonian province. Each time they are closed down, as they travel through Asia Minor in such areas as Galatia and Phrygia. So they keep going, edging toward the northeast into Bithynia (way up to the northeast along the Black Sea) with no success. Now they are forced to backtrack through Mysia (toward the west, along the Sea of Marmara), and they end up on the Mediterranean coast at the port city of Troas.

Here finally Paul receives a preternatural watchword by vision: we must forget about Asia Minor and the Levant, and we must proceed into brand-new foreign territory, into Macedonia and what is beyond on the continent of Europe. The gist of this apparition was Macedonia personified, appealing to him and calling out for Paul's help. How can this be, since Macedonia has not even heard of Jesus, much less been aware of Paul's activities? And why would Macedonia need Paul's help more than Bithynia and Galatia and Phrygia? Considering the missionaries, Paul and Silas and Timothy, this is a surprising development, for Asia Minor is much closer to our temperament, upbringing, and cultural identity.

1.  Consider if God ever tried to get my attention through the inaudible voice of the circumstances and people around me. Anything come to mind? Has it happened more than once?

2.  Reflect on whether I could give up my home and familiar surroundings. What would God have to provide me if I left everything?

> Acts 16:11–15  **11** Setting sail therefore from Troas, we made a direct voyage to Samothrace, and the following day to Neapolis, **12** and from there to Philippi, which is the leading city of the district of Macedonia, and a Roman colony. We remained in this city

---

1. Cf. 2 Tim 1:5; 3:11, 15.

some days; <sup>13</sup> and on the sabbath day we went outside the gate to the riverside, where we supposed there was a place of prayer; and we sat down and spoke to the women who had come together. <sup>14</sup> One who heard us was a woman named Lydia, from the city of Thyatira, a seller of purple goods, who was a worshiper of God. The Lord opened her heart to give heed to what was said by Paul. <sup>15</sup> And when she was baptized, with her household, she besought us, saying, "If you have judged me to be faithful to the Lord, come to my house and stay." And she prevailed upon us.

## Boom Town

More than ever before Paul will run into concentrations of Roman prestige and influence on this side of the Mediterranean Sea. There will be much mixing of civilizations and cultures especially right here on the border of Asia and Europe. The language will change from Greek as second language to Greek as first language. This area is so removed from pockets of Jewish settlers that there is no synagogue around.

At this point of sojourning, our adventure falls into a typical pattern of spiritual experience that I will call "sit, walk, stand." What I mean is that our mission to this strange place goes from conditions of stationary assessment to active efforts toward readiness and fulfillment. You can see this same outlook, Theophilus, if you read your Scriptures—see, for example, how the Psalms begins with a sketch of "sit, walk, stand" in its opening words.[2] What I will do below is give cameos that illustrate each episode of our stay in Philippi.

## Sit

At first, nothing happens. So Paul follows his Jewish instincts and finds along the river—apparently a common gathering space for Diaspora Jews—some women who impulsively know that they must congregate (they "sit," [Acts 16:13]) as Jews if they are to remain faithful. Paul, Silas, and Timothy (and I) meet a businesswoman there from Thyatira (in Asia Minor), and we hit it off splendidly.

2. Psalm 1 has a slightly different configuration. For usage of this dynamic in a Pauline context, see Eph 2:6; 4:1; 6:11.

In the midst of this very conversation, God begins to work. He had shut the doors in Asia Minor and Galatia, revealed a new direction in a vision of the night, drew them to a boom town of new immigrants, and now opens the heart of a woman resident. God shuts and God opens, whether it be passageways to cities or passageways to hearts. It is through these passageways that grace is found for building the Kingdom of God.

Who is Lydia? From the description here she is a transplant from Asia and must have been independent to run her own business. Her baptism on the spot shows that she is decisive, while her unabashed invitation for Paul and his team to stay with her shows her assertiveness. At the end of this Philippi story, she will reappear to offer Paul and Silas her home as a sanctuary when they are released and as a base for Philippi's church to meet. Her positive response leads to her baptism as the first convert in Europe. Paul and the others must have regarded this woman as an open door, for they immediately begin their mission with her.

1. Are there hearts that are open around me who in turn can open the "mission" I am supposed to be doing? How can I recognize them?

2. Am I willing to take chances for God by crossing barriers?

> Acts 16:16–18 **16** As we were going to the place of prayer, we were met by a slave girl who had a spirit of divination and brought her owners much gain by soothsaying. **17** She followed Paul and us, crying, "These men are servants of the Most High God, who proclaim to you the way of salvation." **18** And this she did for many days. But Paul was annoyed, and turned and said to the spirit, "I charge you in the name of Jesus Christ to come out of her." And it came out that very hour.

## Walk

For much of this adventure I was present as eyewitness. I can testify that it was as if Paul and Silas were the main actors and teachers, while Timothy and I were observing as trainees. That is why my Greek narrative is vivid and the action is fast. And if it so happened that I was not on the scene, I interviewed those who were. We will follow Paul and Silas as they walk through the city of Philippi, and I will narrate things as if you and I are beside them.

In this passage, though, what we see is a girl who is used and abused by her operators so that she brings in income. How? Apparently she has the spirit of a "python." This means she has some connection with the supernatural forces of the Pythian oracle, where Apollo defeated the snake god at Delphi. So she can tell the future with her "mantic" clairvoyance. Such a spirit would be connected with death, impurities, and foreboding premonitions. While there is no sure way of knowing what exactly her gifts were, it seems clear that she could go into a trance on the spot (fall down in stupor), could speak in tongues, and that an interpretation would follow to amaze her customers. All these characteristics fall in line with what we know about the oracle at Delphi and its roving mouthpieces.

In this case she recognized something in Paul and Silas like a cosmic changing of the guard—you know, Theophilus, like the Sibyl who announces that Caesar has brought about a new world order (*novus ordo*).[3] Her description of God is typical for Greco-Roman or Persian spirituality, namely, that in the pantheon of gods, there is one (nameless) one who is "most high." Day after day she was attracted to Paul and Silas as opposites attract opposites, as death ultimately stalks and seduces life. She sensed that Paul and Silas were new sources of spiritual gravity in town. She did not enter into the pull of their preaching, only maintaining a safe distance from which she would distract and divide.

Though this dance-step between spiritual centers drew the crowds in Philippi, Paul realized that this confrontation was draining (Acts 16:18, διαπονηθεὶς [*diaponētheis*] a word whose root meaning is "exhaustingly worked out"); and he decides to end this equivocation between "the most high God" and the true God, between the charismatic python spirit and the charismatic Holy Spirit. So he invokes the authority of Christ to bring order and peace to the disruptive woman and to the crowd. The skirmish is brief; the Python influence wanes away within the hour; Paul's voice at least for now is unrivalled.

1. What kind of forces and characters like Python Lady are there around me, chained up but immensely gifted and already involved in a spiritual battle?

2. How do I deal with such forces and people? Who is really in charge?

   Acts 16:22–30 **22** The crowd joined in attacking them; and the magistrates tore the garments off them and gave orders to beat

3. Virgil, *Eclogue* IV.5.

them with rods. **23** And when they had inflicted many blows upon them, they threw them into prison, charging the jailer to keep them safely. **24** Having received this charge, he put them into the inner prison and fastened their feet in the stocks. **25** But about midnight Paul and Silas were praying and singing hymns to God, and the prisoners were listening to them, **26** and suddenly there was a great earthquake, so that the foundations of the prison were shaken; and immediately all the doors were opened and every one's fetters were unfastened. **27** When the jailer woke and saw that the prison doors were open, he drew his sword and was about to kill himself, supposing that the prisoners had escaped. **28** But Paul cried with a loud voice, "Do not harm yourself, for we are all here." **29** And he called for lights and rushed in, and trembling with fear he fell down before Paul and Silas, **30** and brought them out and said, "Men, what must I do to be saved?"

## Stand

This jailer is diligent about his job: he knows that if his prisoners escape—by imperial custom in newly Romanized Philippi—he will be executed and his family will be left forsaken and forlorn. So he puts Paul and Silas into the inner dungeon of the prison, determined that they are now secure. His duty carefully discharged, he nods off to sleep, perhaps amused by his new prisoners' antics.

In the darkest hour of the night, the spirits of Paul and Silas are irrepressible, singing out and praising. Their fellow prisoners also find them a curiosity and even comical. In chains, yet they carry on in merry-making and euphoria!

Now you may ask, Why do these two sing and celebrate? For one thing, in my first account, joy in the midst of persecution is an earmark of discipleship. Remember, for example, the Twelve as they were threatened by the Sanhedrin: "They rejoiced that they were considered worthy to suffer dishonor for the sake of the name" [5:41]. It is an honor to enter into suffering on behalf of Jesus Christ.

For another thing, it is divine intervention that has beckoned Paul and Silas to this continent, to this town, and now even to this very place. Thus, they are shackled in place and rather than hang there waiting for their fate to unfold, they make a *stand* not as victims but as actors in the heavenly courts. Instead of regarding themselves as punished men, they are rewarded men. Now they choose this fate, they celebrate it! The key thing is that they *stand* (not slouch), as performers (not victims) in worship and praise.

To confirm that nothing happens by fluke, now there is a visitation, an earthquake. Earthquakes in themselves are portents that even the most secular of people call "acts of God;" but this is no ordinary earthquake. On one hand, it is so "great" as to shake the prison down to its "foundations;" on the other hand, it possesses the finesse to spring the doors open while keeping everything else intact.

More astonishingly, the severe rumbling only affects one other fixture in the prison: the fetters for each prisoner. They fall off! It unveils an awesomeness of divine visitation and grace, for it is a naked show of power with precise delicacy of effect. For those who have witnessed divine wrath striking in tandem with divine mercy—say an Isaiah [Isa 6:1–7] or a Jacob [Gen 28:16] in the Scriptures—it drives home the need for humility and the call to worship.

This display brings the jailer to a realization of his peril and need for salvation. And what is the jailer's perspective? The jailer awakens and sees his life pass in front of him. Thinking that taking his own life is his only option, he readies his sword for an act of self-sacrifice. Suicide seems to be his only honorable recourse. A divine visitation without divine revelation merely shows the woe and folly of human existence. This raw encounter with cosmic forces draws even an uncultured man like the jailer into cold philosophical calculation.

Instead Paul calls out reassurance and peace in what seems to be chaos and disarray, and the jailer pays heed and sets aside his rash instincts. The divine messenger can speak such grace into the maelstroms of nature, and Paul will do it again later in the story [cf. Acts 27:21–38]. Paul and Silas, therefore, are the agents of grace and peace—and this they demonstrate to us even now as we reimagine the scene.

It dawns on the jailer like light to a blind man: he is the real prisoner and he needs saving! There is no escape from his human nature and predicament except by some intervention. What he has seen and heard from these foreigners, earlier singing and now reassuring, is so captivating, so radiantly charged, that he falls down in trembling before them to find out what he must do.

1. Can I think of times when I have felt chained because of honest decisions I have made that have been misinterpreted? How do I respond

to these times of imprisonment and maybe even veiled threats against my well-being?

2. What can I learn from Paul and Silas's example of singing and thanksgiving in the midst of what seem to be dark circumstances?

3. How am I convinced of my own futility and my need for divine grace to make sense of my circumstances?

4. How am I a divine messenger to those around me? Can I think of a time when God used me as an agent of grace for someone in a crisis?

Acts 16:33–34 <sup>33</sup> And he took them the same hour of the night, and washed their wounds, and he was baptized at once, with all his family. <sup>34</sup> Then he brought them up into his house, and set food before them; and he rejoiced with all his household that he had believed in God.

**Fig. 6: *Paul and Silas in Jail,* by Jamie Treadwell.
Used with the permission of the artist.**

## Sit, Walk, Stand in Philippi

The conviction is so unmistakable that this man needs saving from his own imprisonment, and the light of Paul and Silas so piercing that a new life is possible through their message, that there is no reason to delay entrance into this new life that heaven promises. He is baptized that very night.

In the case of the jailer, his story takes him from a close call with death to an immersion in life. His family, once the sole object of his thoughts and drives, is also baptized and released from their dark cells into infinite light and space. The passage says that the jailer brought Paul and Silas into his house and provided a banquet for them with joy. The Greek word for joy here is an unusual one, signifying "extreme joy" (ἠγαλλιάσατο, ēgalliasato); and the whole household rings out with the same merry-making and euphoria that even chained men can find.

As I think back to the jailer's family and home, is there a hint of both baptism and Eucharist in this moment of grace? For the jailer, held within his own soul's prison, he is now released of his burden and enters into fellowship with Paul and Silas; while he set a table before them, it was himself rather who was fed.[4] And Paul and Silas, so released from responsibility for their seemingly failed ministry in Derbe, sing away the night despite their abuse and their wounds. For they know that by the wounds of Jesus, they all are healed and all prisoners are set free.

This is the story, an eye-witness account of how the Gospel came to a new continent and opened up passageways to the heart of a solitary woman at first, then set free a woman who was enslaved by darkness, and finally opened up the heart of a man who was in his own prison. From the brink of what seemed to be failure and even self-destruction to the heights of joy and salvation, the story of Paul and Silas's mission tells us that the untold purpose of our calling depends on whether we also sit, walk, and stand.

1. Describe any sit, walk, stand experiences I can point to in my life.

2. How do I assess my life right now along these lines?

---

4. "He washed [Paul and Silas] from their stripes and was himself washed from his sins" (John Chrysostom, *Homilies on Acts* 36.2).

# Chapter 17

## Into Achaia (Greece)

### Overview

Let me recollect the itinerary place by place because I think the tedious repetition is needed to explain how we ended up in the heart of the celebrated Greek world called by the ancients "Achaia." Then at the end let us see if I can sum up everything of these travels into this region with some questions.

Our adventure in Philippi only confirmed that we were in the right place—that Paul's vision of Macedonia calling us was divinely appointed. So Paul and the others proceeded into the heart of the country, following the Egnatian Highway, first to Thessalonica, the capital, and then to Beroea. In every new place they would reach out to the Jews first, and then see where the circumstances would lead.

In the case of Thessalonica, they repeatedly went to the synagogue until some of the congregation leaders objected to their message. By then a great many heard Paul and Silas and responded favorably. They reflected the demographics of Philippi: a few Jews, a lot of Greeks, and many independent women. Instead of dealing head-on with the message of Paul and Silas, their opponents stirred up the mobs with fears that these men would turn the world upside down and especially that the Roman Empire itself was threatened. When the uproar escalated into ransacking homes and arbitrary arrests, things got out of control. Yes, to be a Christian now provoked others into turning the world upside down!—and the trio of Paul, Silas, and Timothy knew they could make no more headway in Thessalonica. So, begging leave of "Macedonia Incarnate" who had supplicated

Paul in the first place, they moved on along the Egnatian Highway, certain that they would make good on their plan to return.

> Acts 17:1–9 [1]Now when they had passed through Amphipolis and Apollonia, they came to Thessalonica, where there was a synagogue of the Jews. [2] And Paul went in, as was his custom, and for three weeks he argued with them from the scriptures, [3] explaining and proving that it was necessary for the Christ to suffer and to rise from the dead, and saying, "This Jesus, whom I proclaim to you, is the Christ." [4] And some of them were persuaded, and joined Paul and Silas; as did a great many of the devout Greeks and not a few of the leading women. [5] But the Jews were jealous, and taking some wicked fellows of the rabble, they gathered a crowd, set the city in an uproar, and attacked the house of Jason, seeking to bring them out to the people. [6] And when they could not find them, they dragged Jason and some of the brethren before the city authorities, crying, "These men who have turned the world upside down have come here also, [7] and Jason has received them; and they are all acting against the decrees of Caesar, saying that there is another king, Jesus." [8] And the people and the city authorities were disturbed when they heard this. [9] And when they had taken security from Jason and the rest, they let them go.

The road took them to Beroea. Here, by contrast, the residential Jews were diligent in their Scripture traditions and idealistic in their faith. They took hold of Paul's message week after week. Unfortunately, the rabble-rousers from Thessalonica came to disrupt the progress the trio had made, and Paul was forced to evacuate once again. The other two missionaries, Silas and Timothy, though, stayed behind and helped out anyone who identified with the Kingdom Paul announced; for these citizens could not quite swallow everything that the Thessalonians alleged about the Way. All they could make out from the advance reports was that Paul somehow was poison, but the Beroeans were less susceptible to hearsay and hype.

> Acts 17:10–14 [10] The brethren immediately sent Paul and Silas away by night to Beroea; and when they arrived they went into the Jewish synagogue. [11] Now these Jews were more noble than those in Thessalonica, for they received the word with all eagerness, examining the scriptures daily to see if these things were so. [12] Many of them therefore believed, with not a few Greek women of high standing as well as men. [13] But when the Jews of Thessalonica learned that the word of God was proclaimed by Paul at Beroea also, they came there too, stirring up and inciting the

crowds. **14** Then the brethren immediately sent Paul off on his way
to the sea, but Silas and Timothy remained there.

Nonetheless, Paul was now all alone on a long journey pointing toward Athens. Why they directed him there, I do not know. You know of the reputation of this city: a place hallowed among the Achaeans (Greeks) for its learned academies and intellectual traditions. Paul is no shrinking violet, but among the free-thinkers? Well, it turns out that Paul could hold his own among the poets and philosophers.

He began in the synagogue, as usual, but was quickly drawn out by the open-air and spontaneous discussions held in the city's plaza. Here everyone was free to speak their minds, and generally no opinion was out of bounds. One never knew where public dialogues would end up—they sometimes percolated upward into fresh new thinking, but more often fell into the tar pits of some sophist's eccentricities. Still, the creative potential was enticing brew for anyone who could choke down the initial swig of free-thinking. Paul was man enough for the challenge, but it shook him deeply to see how far afield the human mind could wander.

> Acts 17:16–21 **16** Now while Paul was waiting for them at Athens, his spirit was provoked within him as he saw that the city was full of idols. **17** So he argued in the synagogue with the Jews and the devout persons, and in the market place every day with those who chanced to be there. **18** Some also of the Epicurean and Stoic philosophers met him. And some said, "What would this babbler say?" Others said, "He seems to be a preacher of foreign divinities"—because he preached Jesus and the resurrection. **19** And they took hold of him and brought him to the Areopagus, saying, "May we know what this new teaching is which you present? **20** For you bring some strange things to our ears; we wish to know therefore what these things mean." **21** Now all the Athenians and the foreigners who lived there spent their time in nothing except telling or hearing something new.

He learned quickly: when he saw that his pitch about Jesus rising from the dead was summarily dismissed by the loudest voices, he switched tack and modulated his speech for a better hearing. He had to begin where his audience was—and clearly this crowd in Athens was not the one he encountered in the boondocks of Iconium. Neither, though, were they the biblically literate of Beroea. So he had to appeal to their educated back-grounds while not alienating them with answers so strange as to provoke mockery.

Paul continually surprises, and he did so again. He began his presentation by complimenting them on the art he had noticed in the city and quoting what he remembered from their poetry. You can credit Paul with having a tourist's eye for the statues and temples, but how did he know their poetry? Paul never told us, but I suspect that his wide-ranging mind had already run into the Greek worldview quite a bit in Tarsus, that center of trade and culture on the Asian coast. He had already mixed with people of class and culture growing up there and doing business with them.

In short, he knew what was good and true and noble about them—and to this nature he made his appeal. To appeal especially to the philosophers called the Stoics, he affirmed that the divine was the source of the natural world, not contained by it but separate from it as a being, not simply a force of nature; and it was immaterial in relation to religious institutions and structures. And then to reach out to their rivals called the Epicureans, he quoted of all things their poetry! The verses he cited indicate that God is accessible and can be encountered in nitty-gritty circumstances.

Then, to lay claim to the entire Athenian civic tradition in general, he said that his God was source of the whole human race and its sense of politics; but the order of the seasons and the boundaries of nations all suggest his sovereignty and ownership of this world.

All this without citing the Scriptures! All this without a single reference to Moses! For what good would such formulas derived from these biblical elements be without a proper laboratory to test them? They would be derided and cast aside by junior scientists. Paul knew that the teachings and traditions of his ancestral faith would only fall to the ground on deaf ears in this place.

His speech was a model of moderation and good Greek taste, one that locked into their ways and minds. No baggage that needed to be sorted out, yet carrying the essential truths that would stimulate further investigation into the Way of truth. Yet it ended with a punch: a day of reckoning was coming and somehow it involved the man he had pointed to earlier, a man who had risen from the dead.

Again, this man Jesus! And again, resurrection! This they considered a plunge into the absurd once again. After stroking their Greek sensibilities, Paul ended with these two non-Greek lessons: repentance and resurrection.

Did it win anyone over now? A few perked up as if they understood, and still a few scoffed as if to say, 'Now we've heard it all.' Yet here is the bottom line: one of the fellows well known in these circles grasped and believed. This man became important for the establishment of the local church, and his name became associated with the philosophical abstractions that Athenians are noted for. His name was Dionysius.[1]

> Acts 17:22–34 **22** So Paul, standing in the middle of the Areopagus, said: "Men of Athens, I perceive that in every way you are very religious. **23** For as I passed along, and observed the objects of your worship, I found also an altar with this inscription, 'To an unknown god.' What therefore you worship as unknown, this I proclaim to you. **24** The God who made the world and everything in it, being Lord of heaven and earth, does not live in shrines made by man, **25** nor is he served by human hands, as though he needed anything, since he himself gives to all men life and breath and everything. **26** And he made from one every nation of men to live on all the face of the earth, having determined allotted periods and the boundaries of their habitation, **27** that they should seek God, in the hope that they might feel after him and find him. Yet he is not far from each one of us, **28** for 'In him we live and move and have our being'; as even some of your poets have said, 'For we are indeed his offspring.' **29** Being then God's offspring, we ought not to think that the Deity is like gold, or silver, or stone, a representation by the art and imagination of man. **30** The times of ignorance God overlooked, but now he commands all men everywhere to repent, **31** because he has fixed a day on which he will judge the world in righteousness by a man whom he has appointed, and of this he has given assurance to all men by raising him from the dead." **32** Now when they heard of the resurrection of the dead, some mocked; but others said, "We will hear you again about this." **33** So Paul went out from among them. **34** But some men joined him and believed, among them Dionysius the Areopagite and a woman named Damaris and others with them.

1.  How do I deal with intellectual dissent to my beliefs?

2.  How do I think about the relationship between beauty and God? What is the relationship between art and Jesus? What is my attitude about such things as poetry and philosophy?

---

1. Eusebius, *Ecclesiastical History* III.4.

3. How would I present my interpretation of the truth without use of the Scriptures?

## Further into Achaia (Greece)

Even though Athens was the intellectual hub for the whole Greek world, Corinth was actually the place that Caesar had decided would be the administrative and political capital for the region. So Paul next went here—again by himself. There he learned about two other followers of Jesus whom the emperor had expelled from Rome with many of their fellow Jews due to the arguments regarding whether Jesus really was the messiah. Their names were Aquila and Priscilla, and they were trained in the same trade as Paul, leatherworking. So they set up shop together in Corinth, and their joint operation allowed Paul time on the side to do more outreach among fellow Jews and among the Gentiles.

I picked up my information about Paul from Silas and Timothy who had finally caught up to him in Corinth. They found Paul in the midst of another burst of controversy with the same old club of naysayers found in other synagogues. The idea of a Galilean messiah who died on the cross was a non-starter to them—as it was to so many Jews we encountered everywhere. Paul washed his hands of their hard-heartedness and stomped out. This time, he stayed in town instead of moving on. In fact, he decamped from the synagogue only to set up his preaching headquarters next door! Paul's chutzpah didn't just fade away when he left as at other places. No, this time he stuck around some eighteen months, way longer than most of the places he had heretofore preached.

What made Paul so tenacious in Corinth? First of all, he won over a few of the leading Jews to his interpretations of the Scriptures, and this influenced a few curiosity-seekers present to raise promising questions. But the main reason, I think, was that Paul saw this region just like he saw Macedonia: the Almighty had directly intervened to call him here. Earlier there was that Macedonian apparition who had implored Paul to help, and now the Lord intervened by vision assuring him that everything would be alright and that many Corinthians would receive his testimony.

Even when the synagogue hacks dragged him away to face formal charges before the imperial official for Corinth, the charges were summarily dismissed without even a public hearing. For us, this was an important precedent as well as a confirmation about our mission agenda; for it meant that whatever legal action took place in Rome against Aquila and Priscilla would not happen in the Eastern Empire. The Roman overlords would not be drawn into this quarrel, and instead they expected Jews to work out their own solutions.

> Acts 18:1–3 ¹After this he left Athens and went to Corinth. ² And he found a Jew named Aquila, a native of Pontus, lately come from Italy with his wife Priscilla, because Claudius had commanded all the Jews to leave Rome. And he went to see them; ³ and because he was of the same trade he stayed with them, and they worked, for by trade they were tentmakers.

> Acts 18:5–17 ⁵ When Silas and Timothy arrived from Macedonia, Paul was occupied with preaching, testifying to the Jews that the Christ was Jesus. ⁶ And when they opposed and reviled him, he shook out his garments and said to them, "Your blood be upon your heads! I am innocent. From now on I will go to the Gentiles." ⁷ And he left there and went to the house of a man named Titius Justus, a worshiper of God; his house was next door to the synagogue. ⁸ Crispus, the ruler of the synagogue, believed in the Lord, together with all his household; and many of the Corinthians hearing Paul believed and were baptized. ⁹ And the Lord said to Paul one night in a vision, "Do not be afraid, but speak and do not be silent; ¹⁰ for I am with you, and no man shall attack you to harm you; for I have many people in this city." ¹¹ And he stayed a year and six months, teaching the word of God among them. ¹² But when Gallio was proconsul of Achaia, the Jews made a united attack upon Paul and brought him before the tribunal, ¹³ saying, "This man is persuading men to worship God contrary to the law." ¹⁴ But when Paul was about to open his mouth, Gallio said to the Jews, "If it were a matter of wrongdoing or vicious crime, I should have reason to bear with you, O Jews; ¹⁵ but since it is a matter of questions about words and names and your own law, see to it yourselves; I refuse to be a judge of these things." ¹⁶ And he drove them from the tribunal. ¹⁷ And they all seized Sosthenes, the ruler of the synagogue, and beat him in front of the tribunal. But Gallio paid no attention to this.

1. Do I have a favorable view of work and career in relation to religious mission? How do I use my profession to advance the Kingdom?

2. What is the role of government in the realm of religion? How do I pray for civil authorities?

3. Have I ever been encouraged by direct intervention or revelation of God to do something very hard or controversial? Recall and describe it. How did that divine visitation give me assurance to continue in spite of the difficulty?

## Résumé

Let us catch our breath now by briefly summarizing what Paul has accomplished on this his second journey: Paul's tenacity was remarkable to me, as we saw him stay on in Corinth even after the fracas in front of the proconsul Gallio. Yet even more remarkable to me was that in spite of resistance at every stop along the way, Paul now seemed to have an internal sense that all his travels and efforts had rhythm and coherence.

Thus, Paul conceived of his efforts as weaving together a fabric of relationships that spanned quite different worlds. First, there was the mission to Asia Minor with its wild and woolly ways (Psidian Antioch, Iconium, Derbe, Lystra). Then the Way took him to the more structured and cultured world of Macedonia (Philippi, Thessalonica, Beroea), and circumstances opened up opportunities even farther into Achaea (Athens, Corinth). Finally, and most importantly, Paul could not forget his origins, those who had summoned him and commissioned him to go abroad in the first place (Syrian Antioch and ultimately Jerusalem). These three worlds—Greece, Asia, Israel—were all held together and balanced, somehow, in this man's vision. As events around Paul continued to unfold, even this panorama could not contain his energies, for he would soon tell us that Rome was also in his sights.

In the meantime, Paul related to the obstacles at every juncture as adventures and opportunities. Instead of thinking survival, he was thinking sustainability and success. He lingered here, he fled there; but he always thought in terms of continuity. For example, where were those fresh faces I spoke about—Silas and Timothy, the new generation of leadership that Paul selected to be his traveling partners? Well, when he flees Beroea, they are still in Macedonia shoring up the fledgling initiates.

He departs from Athens, and he leaves Dionysius the Areopagite. He comes alone to Corinth but ends up with Aquila and Priscilla as his new traveling partners in the bigger picture opening up. And he trains them and transplants them to the next destination for Paul: Ephesus, Asia's little Rome. Paul stays briefly here, but long enough to set up something that merits his return to this important city—which I will soon tell you about—and long enough to instruct Aquila and Priscilla to do their own recruiting.

Here Aquila and Priscilla meet Apollos. Apollos represents yet the next wave of outreach, and Aquila and Priscilla set about preparing him for bigger things. Where does Apollos end up? He goes back to Corinth to strengthen what Paul began there. It is like Paul has now three or four generations of spiritual children connected to his efforts on behalf of Kingdom of God.

My point is that Paul has his eyes on the future, recruiting and training workers. He knows the kind of people he wants, and he transplants them in areas that Paul thinks are strategic for how to reach worlds yet unreached. His workers need to know how to move among diverse cultures and populations so that the work can continue without Paul's physical presence. Keep it in mind, Theophilus, and pay attention to how this man's vision leads to his ingenious deployment of resources.

Finally, let me return to Paul's divine summons and commission, for it is the reality that holds Paul's ambition and self-promotion in check. You see Paul's bedrock loyalties when he leaves the mission frontier and resolves to pay what he called a "vow" in the Jerusalem temple. I won't go into the rationale for this vow right now—but I urge you to search the Scriptures to learn more about its origins and its rigors. Let this prospectus of Paul's long-range plan suffice to end my account of his second missionary voyage. To recount some of these key lines in my report:

> Acts 18:1–3 [1]After this he left Athens and went to Corinth. [2] And he found a Jew named Aquila, a native of Pontus, lately come from Italy with his wife Priscilla, because Claudius had commanded all the Jews to leave Rome. And he went to see them; [3] and because he was of the same trade he stayed with them, and they worked, for by trade they were tentmakers.

> Acts 18:18–21 [18] After this Paul stayed many days longer, and then took leave of the brethren and sailed for Syria, and with him Priscilla and Aquila. At Cenchreae he cut his hair, for he had a vow. [19] And they came to Ephesus, and he left them there; but he himself went into the synagogue and argued with the Jews. [20] When they asked him to stay for a longer period, he declined; [21] but on taking leave of them he said, "I will return to you if God wills," and he set sail from Ephesus.

Acts 18:24–28 **24** Now a Jew named Apollos, a native of Alexandria, came to Ephesus. He was an eloquent man, well versed in the scriptures. **25** He had been instructed in the way of the Lord; and being fervent in spirit, he spoke and taught accurately the things concerning Jesus, though he knew only the baptism of John. **26** He began to speak boldly in the synagogue; but when Priscilla and Aquila heard him, they took him and expounded to him the way of God more accurately. **27** And when he wished to cross to Achaia, the brethren encouraged him, and wrote to the disciples to receive him. When he arrived, he greatly helped those who through grace had believed, **28** for he powerfully confuted the Jews in public, showing by the scriptures that the Christ was Jesus.

1. Have I ever met someone who had consuming vision and enthusiasm for execution of that vision? What was my reaction to that person?

2. What role does charisma (such as Paul displays here) play in the growth of the Church? Are there others like him that I can point to in the history of the Church? How can they inspire my life decisions?

3. Do further research to see how Paul's letters might fit the itinerary described above. For example, start paying attention to the names listed above (Silas, Timothy, Apollos, Aquila and Priscilla) and find them in the New Testament elsewhere.

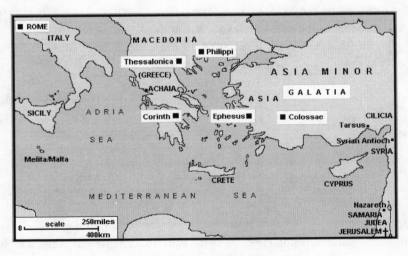

**Fig. 7: Important Cities of Paul's Missionary Travels.**
Used with permission: http://www.ccel.org/bible/phillips/JBPhillips.htm

# Chapter 18

## The Third Journey

Paul's ambition was not to launch new projects and then let them grow on their own. No, he played the role of a parent or nurse, and his projects were really more like organic processes that he nurtured. And if they were so produced by him, then they were also united to those who held Paul accountable. The same homing instinct that drove him to keep coming back to Antioch and Jerusalem motivated him to see the same loyalty generated in his start-up projects. It was this parental solicitude that figured into his every decision about travel and time-investment. Thus, though he had just fulfilled his vow in Jerusalem and taken home leave in Antioch, just as fast he was back on the road. This time, he retraced his first mission in reverse by going first to the backcountry areas and then heading toward the sea.

This third trip established Ephesus, the imperial jewel of Asia Minor, as Paul's new project demanding his attention and devotion. He ended up staying here longer than any other of the places he had targeted for mission—more than two years. You remember that Paul had briefly visited this city and left Aquila and Priscilla to continue the work there. Now he hit the road again to check on them and the progress of the Way there.

Ephesus is an exotic city with a storied past, but Caesar's empire more recently leaves a large footprint there. It is set up like a Roman city with different quadrants for residence and business, a set of buildings and institutions that function in predesigned capacities, an imperial corps of observers, and so on. It has a lot of capital and political patronage invested in it, even though it is not a port on the Mediterranean. Yet this is not simply an imperial client city in Asia either: it has a long history of cooperation with the Greeks going back to Alexander the Great, and the city is famous for passing on Hellenistic culture to the rest of Asia Minor. Less than 200 years ago, its library was the envy of the world—and its temple to Artemis is one of the Seven Wonders. My guess is that you are more under the Ephesian sphere of influence, Theophilus, than any of its rival cities (Alexandria, Antioch, Corinth, etc.), so this current story has a particular relevance for you.

Up to this point, I have told you about the opposition Paul faced from his fellow Jews, especially those who were under the influence of the Jerusalem elites and temple zealots. Even though Paul would win over a few of them through his expert understanding of the Scriptures, in most cases he would stir up an antagonism that would run him out of town or drag him before local authorities to answer for his teachings.

In Ephesus, though, you could meet other types of Jews. One group believed in John the Baptist, for example, the very man about whom I elsewhere have written extensively because he really was the one to clear the Way for Jesus to begin his mission in Palestine. So these folks were already more than open to Paul's perspective. All Paul had to do was hark back to the Baptist's testimony and explain how it was fulfilled. Shortly thereafter they experienced what the Twelve already encountered at Pentecost, namely, special gifts of tongues and prophesying.

A more curious group were itinerant exorcists. If you spend any time among Israelites, whether from Judea or Galilee—or in Samaritan or Diaspora areas, for that matter, as you know from my story about Simon the Magician or Simon Bar-Jesus—you will find individuals who claim the power to "exorcise" or drive out evil spirits. Hopefully you can remember that Jesus had his share of run-ins both with native exorcists and with oppressive demons. I won't try to convince you that evil exists as a roving and self-conscious force that can take up residence in hapless victims. I'm sure that you already have seen cases of oppression in your own land, and certainly we ran into this problem with the Python lady in Philippi.

When Jesus himself instructed his disciples, he said that this exorcism gambit is tricky business and can unleash blowback results if one is not careful. It pits human beings against intelligent and powerful forces. In Ephesus, Paul encountered seven exorcists who were sons of a Jerusalem high priest named Sceva. So far away from their roots and residence, now they were here in Asia Minor! It shows that Jews everywhere were aware of demons and were willing to pay high premiums to keep evil from disrupting the community.

It gets a little comical with these Ephesian exorcists though: They saw how the disciples of Jesus had enviable command over uncontrollable forces of nature and supernature—and thus impressed crowds. So they went around and tried to imitate the disciples by naming Jesus as their patron and protector. In the case of the seven sons of Sceva, one particular demon decided to mock their priestly props. Mere pedigree and pretension do not impress me! the demon asserted. And then it counterattacked and did the reverse of a Kingdom miracle: where cripples leap up in healing and testify to wholeness and health in the great assembly, in this case the poor sons of Sceva, all seven, were jumped by the demoniac and then fled the "house wailing and wounded."

Thrashed and torn apart, their experience only redounded to Paul's glory in Ephesus. Demons know Jesus, and they understand Paul, but Jewish priests as priests are without status in the spiritual realms. What's more, this story only underlined what Jesus once said about the contrast between a house swept clean of evil spirits by a true exorcist and a house in disarray sevenfold after the exorcist's attempt has failed.

> Acts 19:1–9 [1]While Apollos was in Corinth, Paul passed through the interior regions and came to Ephesus, where he found some disciples. [2] He said to them, "Did you receive the Holy Spirit when you became believers?" They replied, "No, we have not even heard that there is a Holy Spirit." [3] Then he said, "Into what then were you baptized?" They answered, "Into John's baptism." [4] Paul said, "John baptized with the baptism of repentance, telling the people to believe in the one who was to come after him, that is, in Jesus." [5] On hearing this, they were baptized in the name of the Lord Jesus. [6] When Paul had laid his hands on them, the Holy Spirit came upon them, and they spoke in tongues and prophesied— [7] altogether there were about twelve of them. [8] He entered the synagogue and for three months spoke out boldly, and argued persuasively about the kingdom of God. [9] When some stubbornly refused to believe and spoke evil of the Way before the congregation, he left them, taking the disciples with him, and argued daily in the lecture hall of Tyrannus.

1. Is there an invisible world of evil spirits? Offer any evidence, personal or anecdotal, for this supernatural world. Is exorcism or deliverance possible today? What in the story above implies that caution must be exercised in encounters with such forces?

2. How can I get a better reading on the difference between "quasi-Christian" beliefs, that is, doctrines or dogmas that lack depth of theology and a full understanding of historic Church positions? Is there any insight to be gained from the example of the Ephesian followers of John the Baptist or from seven sons of Sceva?

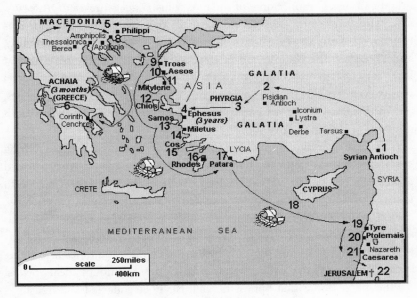

**Fig. 8: Paul's Third Voyage.**
Used with permission: http://www.ccel.org/bible/phillips/JBPhillips.htm

## Two Worlds

Let me not get too far ahead of myself. Even before the street-level Ephesians saw what happened to the seven sons, Paul already had some kind of cult hero status. I mean, even his personal garments become sources of healing energy for others. Of course you and I understand that his power stems from dedication to his divine calling and not from occultic sources, as even the aforementioned demons say that they recognize Paul in light of Jesus. Conversion is the take-away Paul offers to the people in the streets of Ephesus, not special powers stemming from the world of magic.

Everybody saw what happened to the sons of Sceva. But more than laughing at priestly and pretentious power-seekers, they now trembled a bit for themselves. You see, Ephesus was not just a center of exoteric culture, it also was a vortex of esoteric instruction, the magic arts that claimed to give practitioners access to the unseen world of spells, trances, and spirits.

Again, I don't have to tell you that even the most rational person or teacher often displays a streak of irrationality and submission to what we might call superstition. Some of the most illustrious geniuses of history— say, Pythagoras—are also the quirkiest. In the mythological world, it is envisioned as the struggle between Apollo, the civilized god of rationality, and Dionysus, the chaotic god of irrationality, both of whom resided at legendary Delphi on Mount Parnassus. All of us pay lip service to both gods in our everyday life, that is, we are a mix of irrational and rational drives; but in this case, Paul's testimony to Jesus and the Kingdom shakes both domains of Delphi's native sons.

At first, everyone simply recognized that Jesus represented something stronger than any god they had ever heard about. Then as they learned more, they realized that if they actually believed in Jesus, they needed to follow him along the Way that Paul walked. According to this new teaching, esoterica and its stash of secrets were only evidence of a massive failure to submit to the one God. This One cannot be manipulated by dark incantations and magical rituals, but only by heartfelt confession to Jesus as intercessor. Again I say that conversion was Paul's message, not magical powers. All the magic books that Ephesian occultists once collected and treasured were now rendered vain and even harmful to those on the Way with Paul, Aquila, Priscilla, and Apollos. The result? The erstwhile practitioners now came forward, renounced their ways and burned their books at tremendous loss to their finances and fortunes.

## Excursus

Let me bring forward a magician's perspective on Paul's arrival in Ephesus. For him his coming was like an epiphany expressed in the poem I obtained below:

### Magician's Prayer

> Teach me, O Muses, what lore I never sought
> Till Saul, wandering Jew, "God-spell" was brought.
> Its word hit deeper than secrets clandestinely prized,
> Saul's holy book than truths my magic disguised.

Teach me, O Muses, what this book doth reveal
Not "abracadabra," not by snake-charm's deal.
No, this Saul tells such stories from faraway places,
How holy bids chasteness, and grace brightens faces.

Such fierceness, like sun that bleaches harsh stone;
Such softness, like showers to douse bloom's cologne.
He brings power and wisdom in his book from of old;
Nothing from it beams, but in light and in bold.

So, Muses, how can I keep both books, both sides?
One would stir me to preach, the other to hide.
One binds me with cords drawn, all too tight;
The other so strange, and thrilling its height.

I have taken my stand; I will burn all my books,
And destroy, once for all, their guiles, traps, and hooks.
And though I know not the end of Bible's demands,
I'll search it all through, clutched closely in hands.

The thing I found fascinating was their response to Paul's message:
Rather than selling their books and using the proceeds to advance some
charitable cause—maybe even allowing Paul to do more teaching and less
tent-making—they *burned* their books. As near as I can tell, they did so for
two reasons. First, they gleaned from the writings of Moses that all traces
of magic must be devoted to total incineration.[1] Paul must have had private
parleys with these practitioners on this hot-button issue in his two years at
Ephesus. Otherwise, it would not make much sense to burn them.

Second, the value of these books—I was told it was 50,000 silver
coins—seems to have expressed how heartfelt was the initial dedication
these fellows felt toward the Way. For them it was like an offering of immense
worth to consecrate their resolve. Remember the woman who poured out
precious perfume on the feet of Jesus? Was it a waste on Jesus? Both the
woman and these fellows counted perfume and books as nothing in comparison to their devotion, but it was in the act of pouring out or burning
that they confirmed their zeal. For them, such losses sustained are better
viewed as investments in monuments that testify to their commitments.

---

1. Deut 18:10–14.

Acts 19:11–17 **11** And God did extraordinary miracles by the hands of Paul, **12** so that handkerchiefs or aprons were carried away from his body to the sick, and diseases left them and the evil spirits came out of them. **13** Then some of the itinerant Jewish exorcists undertook to pronounce the name of the Lord Jesus over those who had evil spirits, saying, "I adjure you by the Jesus whom Paul preaches." **14** Seven sons of a Jewish high priest named Sceva were doing this. **15** But the evil spirit answered them, "Jesus I know, and Paul I know; but who are you?" **16** And the man in whom the evil spirit was leaped on them, mastered all of them, and overpowered them, so that they fled out of that house naked and wounded. **17** And this became known to all residents of Ephesus, both Jews and Greeks; and fear fell upon them all; and the name of the Lord Jesus was extolled.

Acts 19:18–20 **18** Many also of those who were now believers came, confessing and divulging their practices. **19** And a number of those who practiced magic arts brought their books together and burned them in the sight of all; and they counted the value of them and found it came to fifty thousand pieces of silver. **20** So the word of the Lord grew and prevailed mightily.

1. Were there priorities that I had earlier in life that changed when I became a follower of Jesus? What happened to the old priorities? Do they still have any hold?

2. What things are in my life right now that threaten my relationship with God? How can I make these things a "trophy" to God?

3. Is there a comparison between the Bible and other books? What does this passage teach about the usefulness of knowledge and book learning in relation to the Bible? What books might be downright inimical to the Bible?

# Chapter 19

## Lost in Translation

I am glad that you can read my Greek, Theophilus, and not just listen to popularized reports. Sometimes the message I intended is garbled by the messenger, and I am afraid that a certain obfuscation occurred when I continued my narrative after the events surrounding the miracles and wonders at Ephesus. What I said was Ὡς δὲ ἐπληρώθη ταῦτα (*Hōs de eplērōthē tauta*); and of course you know that this phrase points to a "fulfillment" process at work, not simply "after these events" [19:21]—despite how the passage reads below. The literal meaning is "when these things were fulfilled." To put it somewhat differently, the sense of my words is that something is falling into place. Paul was increasingly aware of the bigger picture—as mentioned above. Certainly the Way that Paul and others are following is leading to a definite end, and Paul glimpses it increasingly in his travels.

The second phrase I used—usually overlooked by the reader—that clues you into the sense of anticipation that follows Paul—is the phrase the dumbed-down version articulates as "about that time"(in Greek: κατὰ τὸν καιρὸν ἐκεῖνον, *kata ton kairon ekeinon* [19:23]). You can see for yourself that I mean "the right time," that is, a moment of destiny or a seasonal fulfillment. 'At that critical moment,' we might paraphrase the Greek. You should sense momentousness stealing its way into my story—and be aware of remarkable timing.

So I was trying to make you aware that things are often not what they seem. Certainly this is not news to you if you have been paying attention especially to what I have said about Paul's deployments and travel plans. Yet it is acutely necessary to hold on to this perspective as I narrate to you what happened next in this place. After so much publicity and success in

Ephesus, now controversy and trials would arise from sources not usually riled up by the Way.

> Acts 19:21–23 **21**Now after these events Paul resolved in the Spirit to pass through Macedonia and Achaia and go to Jerusalem, saying, "After I have been there, I must also see Rome." **22** And having sent into Macedonia two of his helpers, Timothy and Erastus, he himself stayed in Asia for a while. **23** About that time there arose no little stir concerning the Way.

1. Describe an incident where miscommunication has led to completely different results than what was expected.

2. Give an example where I have been a part of something much bigger than myself. What role did I play? How necessary was I to the eventual outcome?

## Reversal

Ephesus is not only an imperial center for the Eastern Mediterranean but something like a pilgrimage destination for devotees of the goddess Artemis. Her temple there is an imposing site, one of the Seven Wonders of the World, and it draws visitors from all over. When they come, they bring their hopes and dreams and superstitions, and—best of all for native Ephesians—their money.

It is this intersection of devotion, money, and the Way, where Paul and his workers run into trouble. The whole mission at Ephesus, otherwise so stunningly successful, was suddenly at risk. Before this moment it seemed that nothing could hinder the coming of the Kingdom of God, just as the earliest disciples had imagined at the opening of my book. 'No,' the Spirit of Jesus seems to answer. When it looks like he is triumphantly risen from the dead, it is not the time or season that you otherwise think. Great reversals will yet happen, and things are not as they seem.

The Kingdom, as Paul represents it, must necessarily clash with the popular Ephesian understanding of Artemis. In this case, the "handlers" of Artemis's reputation are worried that they will lose business if Paul's Kingdom catches on. Pilgrimage is a big money-maker for Ephesus. Paul threatens it, and a lot of push-back comes from power-brokers in the system.

Look at things from Paul's perspective: he and his followers started thinking that maybe their whole mission would go up in smoke—just like the magic books burned in public testimony of the magicians' conversion. Everybody loving Paul now will soon become everyone hating Paul. Now Paul must show his detachment to the precious things of life—not gold or prestige can compare to his commitment to the Way.

However, things are not always as they seem . . .

> Acts 19:24–28 **24** For a man named Demetrius, a silversmith, who made silver shrines of Artemis, brought no little business to the craftsmen. **25** These he gathered together, with the workmen of like occupation, and said, "Men, you know that from this business we have our wealth. **26** And you see and hear that not only at Ephesus but almost throughout all Asia this Paul has persuaded and turned away a considerable company of people, saying that gods made with hands are not gods. **27** And there is danger not only that this trade of ours may come into disrepute but also that the temple of the great goddess Artemis may count for nothing, and that she may even be deposed from her magnificence, she whom all Asia and the world worship." **28** When they heard this they were enraged, and cried out, "Great is Artemis of the Ephesians!"

1.  Have I ever seen a complete reversal of fate for people or events? Give an example and describe the reaction of those who were impacted?

2.  How do business and religion work hand-in-hand? Give an example in life or history.

## Publicity and Religion

Demetrius is a big entrepreneur: he builds domestic shrines out of silver for pious tourists and he provides work for a lot of subcontractors. He is a city-wide mover and shaker in addition to being a successful business man. He correctly assesses the ultimate implications of Paul's ideas: temples have no particular divine value in themselves. (We already saw this keynote in Stephen's bold testament to his furious audience [Acts 6].) Even more radically Paul teaches that any human artifice of divinity is suspect—and he has said as much when he addressed the Athenians and their slogan "to an unknown god" (17:23).

Note how almost every point of Demetrius's assessment of the Way is accurate: Paul's reputation now is spreading all over Asia and he is an influence on the multitude; his preaching signals that Demetrius's business will be "scrutinized" or "investigated" (εἰς ἀπελεγμὸν, *eis apelegmon* [Acts

19:27]). The result Demetrius points to is that Ephesus will lose its status as a pilgrimage city for Artemis. And finally this will undo the whole universe as Ephesus knows it. The Status Quo will be profoundly changed by Paul's gospel.

So what does Demetrius do? He starts a publicity campaign of disinformation. The word I use for this process is "confusion" (συγκεχυμένη, sugkechymenē [Acts 19:32]). Why is this word so interesting? It is the same root word for "formation," but with a different prefix to negate the root. It is the word that describes Apollos's instruction in the faith (κατηχημένος, katēchēmenos [Acts 18:25]). The cognate for it is "catechumenate," and you will increasingly encounter this word as we instruct people about the faith implications of our testimony. Thus, Demetrius begins a "deformation" program utilizing word of mouth, the theater, the public's desire for scandal, and human inclination for panic. He is a mastermind of smearing people, and he knows a very clever way to counteract truth. If Paul and his discipleship methods threaten to turn the city upside down via their catechumenate program, then Demetrius can do the same in reverse.

How quickly disinformation and slander can turn around the reputation of public figures! I am sure that you can come up with your own list of famous people who once commanded everyone's attention and are now in the dustbin of history. Everybody loves celebrity's success, and everyone loves celebrity's scandal; the pendulum just depends on the latest news.

> Acts 19:29–34 **29** So the city was filled with the confusion; and they rushed together into the theater, dragging with them Gaius and Aristarchus, Macedonians who were Paul's companions in travel. **30** Paul wished to go in among the crowd, but the disciples would not let him; **31** some of the Asiarchs also, who were friends of his, sent to him and begged him not to venture into the theater. **32** Now some cried one thing, some another; for the assembly was in confusion, and most of them did not know why they had come together. **33** Some of the crowd prompted Alexander, whom the Jews had put forward. And Alexander motioned with his hand, wishing to make a defense to the people. **34** But when they recognized that he was a Jew, for about two hours they all with one voice cried out, "Great is Artemis of the Ephesians!"

1. How does this passage illustrate how the "Way" scrutinizes culture and critiques it?

2. What ought to be the relationship between religion and society today? Some models proposed have been that religion should be totally independent, within, against, or for society. What light does this passage give on these models?

3. Give examples of how public relations efforts have determined the success or failure of products or elections. Give examples of how they ruined or saved reputations or business ventures.

4. What ought to be our (or the Church's) response to the use of publicity or the media?

## Pulling Strings

The final point to notice in this whole Ephesian dust-up is the role of law and order. Don't overlook, Theophilus, what I tacitly support: a view of reality dependent on the rule of law and government. Remember how vital the proconsul Gallio [Acts 18:12–17] was to the believers in Corinth when he refused to be drawn into interreligious wrangling. He made no overt effort to stop Paul's preaching or his training of new workers for the Way. Even earlier, in Philippi, the city officials do not really want to hurt Paul, and their treatment of him was only because of their ignorance of his Roman credentials [Acts 16:37–40]. In this present episode, it is the Asiarchs who successfully advise Paul to take a low profile. They are not even believers, only Roman monitors in imperial cities who side with their fellow citizen Paul.

Notice, too, it is the town clerk who keeps things under control. People on the street need law and order, and the clerk successfully coaxes citizens to return to daily life routines. If the people are "quiet and do nothing rash," peaceful conditions will return that are more conducive to the Way. Ironic, isn't it, that Demetrius's strategy has been stymied by what would appear to be the Kingdom of God's archrival in the visible world, the Roman Empire? I leave you to ponder this strange alliance.

Indeed, what the clerk says is true about Paul: he is not sacrilegious (ἱεροσύλους [*hierosylous*] a word that means a "temple robber") and also not a blasphemer of Artemis. In the strict sense of the words, Paul has done neither crime, and otherwise seems law-abiding. The official assumes that Demetrius has no case—and certainly, Theophilus, we can have a clear conscience as we give testimony in public: we do not make it our aim to tear down rivals and reputations. The courts, the law, the proconsul, all of these institutions mean that Paul and we have allies in high places. We do not represent a revolutionary force except in the long-term view of history.

> Acts 19:35–41 **35** And when the town clerk had quieted the crowd, he said, "Men of Ephesus, what man is there who does not know that the city of the Ephesians is temple keeper of the great Artemis, and of the sacred stone that fell from the sky? **36** Seeing then that these things cannot be contradicted, you ought to be quiet and do nothing rash. **37** For you have brought these men here who are neither sacrilegious nor blasphemers of our goddess. **38** If therefore Demetrius and the craftsmen with him have a complaint against any one, the courts are open, and there are proconsuls; let them bring charges against one another. **39** But if you seek anything further, it shall be settled in the regular assembly. **40** For we are in danger of being charged with rioting today, there being no cause that we can give to justify this commotion." **41** And when he had said this, he dismissed the assembly.

1. What times in the past have people in high places pulled strings for me or my family? Give examples.

2. What ought to be the role of government or rulers in the defense of individual rights or unpopular causes? Give some examples of how government or rulers did or did not intervene.

3. How have and have not governments and rulers safeguarded religion?

# Chapter 20

## On the Road Again

This was the end of the line for Paul in Ephesus. He could never go back there after Demetrius had ruined his reputation among the rank and file Ephesians. All of what Paul has done in the last three years seems to hang in the balance, as presumably the church tried to take a lower profile— and Paul is forced to seek refuge elsewhere. As Paul had learned over the course of his travels, sometimes one should stay and fight and sometimes one should cut the losses and flee. He left Ephesus, but was confident that the church there was on a good foundation and in the hands of people he trusted.

He made a quick turn about Macedonia and Achaea, visiting the string of churches he had founded and organized. These included the ones I have already featured: Philippi, Thessalonica, Beroea, Athens, and Corinth. In Corinth he committed more of his time, spending some three months there trying to iron out his relationship with their leaders. To compound his miseries, the Jews of Greece had not forgotten their hostility toward him and fomented a plot to attack him on his return trip to Syria. To throw them off, he made a snap decision to return by the long route through Macedonia and around the northern rim of the Aegean Sea.

Even though Paul had his share of woes as he visited his groups, just consider the liveliness and loyalty he had fostered in his band of traveling companions from the four corners of his mission: there was Sopater from Beroea, Aristarchus and Secundus from Thessalonica, Gaius from Derbe, Timothy from Lystra, Tychicus and Trophimus from Asia Minor. Paul could depend on these fellows as rough and ready delegates to each place he worked. This does not even count his older associates at Ephesus (Aquila and Priscilla) and his more independent supporters in Achaea (Dionysius and Apollos). I tell you, Paul always had his mind on the strategic advantages of recruitment and resources. And undoubtedly this close-knit cadre served as consolation and companionship in all his troubles.

> Acts 20:4 He was accompanied by Sopater son of Pyrrhus from Beroea, by Aristarchus and Secundus from Thessalonica, by Gaius from Derbe, and by Timothy, as well as by Tychicus and Trophimus from Asia.

1. How much fellowship and encouragement do I get from the people around me? Do I make it a priority to find and spend time with supportive colleagues and friends? Why or why not?

2. Give an example of a friend or a circle of supporters who made all the difference for me when I faced tough times.

3. Consider once again the wide scope of the divine call and election. How do I foster within myself a sense of ecumenism?

## Troas

We all met up again at Troas on the first day of the week. It was this port city where Paul had the vision of Macedonia itself calling for help, and now the disciples gathered together at nightfall to bid farewell to Paul. According to the Jewish reckoning of time, the night brought on Sunday, and vigils for Shabbat and first day of the week now were *de rigueur* for many Jews. We were all gathered together to pay tribute to Paul, to hear him speak, and then to break bread. The latter ceremony you might recognize from something called "Eucharist," a reenactment of the last time Jesus spent with the Twelve.

It is remarkable that Paul's brief time in Troas had born such fruit over the years. The whole upper room was so full that people were sitting in the window sills overlooking the atrium where Paul spoke. I suspect that such displays of support for Paul show that the Troatians thought that that this might be the last time they would see Paul.

The young man Eutychus was among them, though he was seated high on the third floor balcony. Having done his Jewish Shabbat prayers in the morning, he was now worn out and nodded off to sleep as Paul's sermon went on. All of a sudden he fell from that window onto the street below. Paul interrupted his speech to check up on the lad and perhaps to channel the healing power of God into him. By the time Paul finished the Eucharist and finished his conversation with them at daybreak (!), the lad Eutychus was recovered.

## Revery

As I think back, something tells me that such nights are but a respite, when time seems to stop in breathless anticipation. What can I say that will not lessen the awe of that short spell in Troas? Better for me to wax silent, Theophilus, and for you to ponder its soft voice: Awake all night, absorbed in Paul's last act at Troas, a performance which had begun with a nocturnal eloquence and ended with such a miracle! All this dawned upon us during this magic interval between the last day and the first day of the week, as the lamps burned all night with supernatural aura in this make-shift sanctuary. We sensed heaven's infusion during Paul's speaking. All I can say is that we hung on his every word and savored every crumb of bread broken. Yes, it was the first day of a new week as if the world were created again, and Troas was invited to start things over.

## What Do You Tell Us, Eutychus?

Eutychus,
Truly a song crowns your name,[1]
Through the ages the meaning is sung:
For your name is a story that ends up in glory.
Arise, take life, the dawn is begun.

Eutychus,
Once you yawned at spent labors,
As seventh day could not restore the week.
Earth tries to make show and take leave of its woe;
Until now when a new day would speak.

1. "Eutychus" in Greek means "fortunate one" or "lucky one."

Eutychus,
Did you miss of Paul's meaning and word,
As he spun away the night with tales?
Did you miss in your fall, the point of it all—
Bread broken and heavenly regales?

Eutychus,
While you dozed in such a state,
Braced were we with power and vision
Of life that was past, yet new one to last:
Between both, your grace-filled collision!

Eutychus,
Now listen and start out afresh,
For now the world of yesterday is dead;
Pay heed to your fame, for "Luck" is your name,
And Fate for all is turned on its head.

Eutychus,
Young man, teach us the lesson,
Teach the young about Kingdom and power;
And your lesson let swell to elders as well,
Aslumber they be because of the hour.

Eutychus,
The dawn is now come, and Paul is away,
Eutychus, come out of your deadly trance!
For Troatians the joy to recover the boy;
But for you the gift of second chance.

Reader,
Think now of names I've twice given:
"Eutychus" and "Theophilus"[2] above.
In them God is laughter to ward off disaster,
First day, new week, Kingdom love!


2. "Theophilus" in Greek means "lover of God."

Acts 20:7–12 <sup>7</sup> On the first day of the week, when we were gathered together to break bread, Paul talked with them, intending to depart on the morrow; and he prolonged his speech until midnight. <sup>8</sup> There were many lights in the upper chamber where we were gathered. <sup>9</sup> And a young man named Eutychus was sitting in the window. He sank into a deep sleep as Paul talked still longer; and being overcome by sleep, he fell down from the third story and was taken up dead. <sup>10</sup> But Paul went down and bent over him, and embracing him said, "Do not be alarmed, for his life is in him." <sup>11</sup> And when Paul had gone up and had broken bread and eaten, he conversed with them a long while, until daybreak, and so departed. <sup>12</sup> And they took the lad away alive, and were not a little comforted.

1. Have I ever had a sense that I would never see someone or do something again? What reaction did it cause in me?

2. Have I found myself sleeping or inattentive at key moments of history or progress? What trouble did it land me in when I could not maintain presence of mind?

3. Have I ever been a part of a once-in-a-lifetime event that still resonates in memory as if it happened yesterday? Was God involved? How?

## Rites of Passage

I hope you can glimpse that events seem to unfold around Paul like choreography, and we all simply accompanied him in the dance. On one hand, the work week and the Shabbat were recalibrated according to the Kingdom; and then on the other hand, the arrangement of days only led into seasons of fulfillment.

What do I mean by the latter? Well, there is a pulse to Israel's calendar that roughly follows the agricultural seasons, yet this arrangement carries with it a deeper meaning for cycles of nature. As you study the Scriptures, you can sense this more and more. However, what I am also suggesting is that the cycles of human activities also unfold to the Almighty in calendar correspondence. Let us call these ebbs and flows of time the *kairos* ("critical") moments; they charge up the natural year with meaning, and we can plot Paul on this seasonal continuum.

So as Paul leaves Troas, it is perhaps three or four weeks past Israel's feast of Unleavened Bread (Passover) and nearing Pentecost. You remember that what brought back Paul to Jerusalem earlier was his concern to fulfill a vow. Now Paul, becoming more cognizant of the calendar, expresses his desire to return again to Jerusalem to celebrate the harvest feast of Pentecost. He senses that he has reached the end of his course here in the Eastern Mediterranean. Three times around Asia Minor, Macedonia, and Achaea, and something new is ahead for him. If Pentecost is the harvest feast, so his mission has reached its seasonal fulfillment.

> Acts 20:16–17 [16] For Paul had decided to sail past Ephesus, so that he might not have to spend time in Asia; he was eager to be in Jerusalem, if possible, on the day of Pentecost. [17] From Miletus he sent a message to Ephesus, asking the elders of the church to meet him.

1. Have I ever been absorbed in a project and sensed it was time to move on? How did I know? What happened when I stopped or continued my efforts?

2. How does my faith go through seasons? How can I be more in tune with God's timing?

3. What are some of the rites of passage that correspond to the seasons of life? What personal observances mark changes in my life? Should I observe such rites in these seasons? What rites can I implement for these times? How can I make these passage times more dedicated to God?

## Paul's Testament

His inner compass set on finishing one thing and beginning another, Paul determines to make a final address to the group he has spent most time with and perhaps loves most dearly: the elders of Ephesus. He meets them at Miletus, a safe distance from the source of the earlier melee. Three years of work had blown up in Paul's face as Demetrius and his rabble-rousing clientele precipitated the crisis. The combination of the public furor and Paul's removal from his Ephesus project a dark hue onto the speech which I excerpt below. In his address, Paul directly tells his audience that he is sure that he will never again return to Ephesus—and so the address reads like a last will and testimony. Tied up with this compact résumé of his words are many of the themes to epitomize Paul's sense of identity and mission.

What he told the elders was that he personally experienced severe trials and sorrows in their midst, even though they (and I) might not have noticed. My narrative initially did not expose Paul's inner turmoils, though in my retelling below I try to imagine how any human being would be discouraged at the turn of events he experienced. In heart-to-heart fashion he tells them that his service brought humility and tears and trials because of the opposition he faced (20:19). He "did not shrink from"—in Greek ὑπεστειλάμην (hypesteilamēn) a word that implies internal collapse or defeat—his duties as the Lord's servant.

How did Paul maintain his equilibrium? For one thing, there was his sense that ownership belonged to Another: he was only a servant or steward of the Lord, not owner of or investor in the project. You pick this idea up, Theophilus, when he uses the term you have heard me cite repeatedly, "Kingdom," implying that Paul is merely its herald. He also addresses the elders in terms of shepherd and flock, suggesting ownership by someone other. I believe that these terms were comforting to Paul, and they should be comforting to both of us because it relieves us of the final responsibilities for success.

Another thing that seemed to help Paul was his sense of accountability: ultimately he reported to the Lord, not to the mission or its beneficiaries. Notice, for example, how he says he is "serving the Lord"—not Ephesus or its elders. Later he speaks about "credit" that he and the elders cannot take or give. Why? Because it is the Lord Jesus who assigns value, and thus Paul implies his value as worker is only what the King or the owner assigns him. Later in this testament, he maintains that his organizational talent, his miracle-working, and his sermons all fall short of taking ultimate responsibility for the mission.

The fulfillment theme I mentioned just above comes out when Paul says his aim is to "accomplish my course and the ministry which I received from the Lord Jesus." This phrase means that he has a δρόμος (dromos, a race or a course that is prearranged or laid out, presumably by divine providence). Paul is only a participant in a grandly designed operation—he has a role, but the outcome is beyond his reach.

Look at how he addresses his Ephesian audience as "overseers," an office that implies that someone else is owner and employer. Paul did not choose them as much as confirm them, and they did not set themselves up as overseers. The word itself only affirms that these elders are in reality not owners but more like stand-ins for the owner: Yes, they must guard and tend, but the tragic losses among the sheep are not ultimately theirs to sustain. Sheep ravaged by wolves belong neither to shepherds nor to nature, but to the owner.

Within that same statement of Paul is the reason for divine ownership of the whole operation of mission, sheep, and shepherds: God has purchased it through his own blood (Acts 20:28 περιεποιήσατο διὰ τοῦ αἵματος τοῦ ἰδίου [periepoiēsato dia tou haimatos tou idiou]). Something has been again lost in the translation, Theophilus, for most render this passage with the insertion of "Son," but my words at best imply this notion. Rather, what I said suggests that God's own blood has been sufficient for claim of ownership.

I realize that this transmission may make many unhappy with its vagueness, but I want you to ponder divine ownership for the Church and your responsibility for it. We often say that "blood, sweat, and tears" go into something we prize, and I think we can extrapolate this saying into the realm of divine care for the church at Ephesus. Such a cost has involved Paul's blood, sweat, and tears—but this cost is expected from everyone involved in the project. Remember that earlier Saul was persecuting Jesus when he went after the believers at Damascus—their suffering was his, their blood was his. The main point of the speech, though, is that the Church belongs to God and not to Paul, the overseers, or anything else.

This basic presupposition undergirds Paul's speech. It means that Paul can let go, in spite of all the exhaustive labor he has done in Ephesus. The work was arduous and costly: it took three years; he worked day and night; he wept over the work (all this is in 20:31); he worked at his expense (20:34). And yet the bottom line of this speech is its conclusion: "And now I commend you to God and to the word of his grace, which is able to build you up and to give you the inheritance among all those who are sanctified."

Why does he end his speech with the famous last words, "It is more blessed to give than to receive"? Certainly he can do no wrong by quoting Jesus (though these exact words he must have picked up from a source I do not know). However, I think that in the end Paul's philosophy of life is to not pay attention to the returns on investment but to the investing. The surrender and sacrifice of his life's efforts so evident in his testament that God is owner ultimately of everything and God's own great generosity—purchasing the Church "with his own blood"—is the model for any missionary of the Gospel. Jesus's life proves the wisdom of the maxim he quotes: seemingly wasted, now in God's hands for safekeeping; once lavishly poured out, now preciously collected as ointment.

Acts 20:18–35 **18** And when they came to him, he said to them: "You yourselves know how I lived among you all the time from the first day that I set foot in Asia, **19** serving the Lord with all humility and with tears and with trials which befell me through the plots of the Jews; **20** how I did not shrink from declaring to you anything that was profitable, and teaching you in public and from house to house, **21** testifying both to Jews and to Greeks of repentance to God and of faith in our Lord Jesus Christ. **22** And now, behold, I am going to Jerusalem, bound in the Spirit, not knowing what shall befall me there; **23** except that the Holy Spirit testifies to me in every city that imprisonment and afflictions await me."

**24** But I do not account my life of any value nor as precious to myself, if only I may accomplish my course and the ministry which I received from the Lord Jesus, to testify to the gospel of the grace of God. **25** And now, behold, I know that all you among whom I have gone preaching the kingdom will see my face no more. **26** Therefore I testify to you this day that I am innocent of the blood of all of you, **27** for I did not shrink from declaring to you the whole counsel of God.

**28** Take heed to yourselves and to all the flock, in which the Holy Spirit has made you overseers, to care for the church of God which he obtained with the blood of his own Son. **29** I know that after my departure fierce wolves will come in among you, not sparing the flock; **30** and from among your own selves will arise men speaking perverse things, to draw away the disciples after them. **31** Therefore be alert, remembering that for three years I did not cease night or day to admonish every one with tears.

**32** And now I commend you to God and to the word of his grace, which is able to build you up and to give you the inheritance among all those who are sanctified. **33** I coveted no one's silver or gold or apparel. **34** You yourselves know that these hands ministered to my necessities, and to those who were with me. **35** In all things I have shown you that by so toiling one must help the weak, remembering the words of the Lord Jesus, how he said, 'It is more blessed to give than to receive.'"

1. How would I sum up my life in two paragraphs? Try to do so now.

2. What would be the last thing I would want to tell those who are my dependents?

3. What is the "course" and the ministry that the Lord has given to me?

4. What ownership do I have for things that take my time and attention?

5. If I am only a caretaker, how does this offer me release from worries? How much do I pay attention to what others think of my life and decisions? How am I influenced by what others reckon of my performance?

6. How did Paul relate to the worth of his life? What does he say about the significance of his own service and his life?

7. How can I take the approach that it is more "blessed to give than to receive?" Can I keep giving when I am not recognized?

# Chapter 21

## Don't Go, Don't Go!

Don't go, don't go, they urged, as we made our way through waterways and highways to Jerusalem. Each group got wind of Paul's return trip and gathered to bid farewell to him. Paul, though, was heedless of any pleading: his path led inexorably to some fulfillment that not even dire prophecy could deflect.

The thing that struck me about the welcoming crowds were their new faces. Yes, there were some old-timers that link the beginning of my memoirs to the end, but there were budding start-up groups and fresh-faced second and third generation leaders at most of these places. The Way was changing and adapting to a world where the Twelve were only known through the Apostolic Decree and through stories passed down about such things as the Pentecost experience and the outbreak of persecutions against them. Paul, who had not seen Jesus himself, now meets with many others who also did not personally meet Jesus, even as he enters the native land of the One whom they all venerate.

One of his familiar stops along the way was Caesarea. Here we run into the remnants of that former transitionary leadership team called the Seven, specifically Philip. They called him "the Evangelist" because of his preaching and adventures among the Samaritans and his miraculous encounter with the treasurer from Ethiopia, both of which cleared the Way to a universal vision of the Kingdom.

Philip the Evangelist had settled down in Caesarea and had passed on his soaring spirit to his four unmarried daughters. They were known throughout Judea as prophetesses. They, together with other prophets along the way, were convinced that Paul was running a gauntlet of dangerous pitfalls which could only end up in his demise. Paul, never one to squelch supernatural guidance, patiently listened but decided that he would not turn aside from the trajectory ("the course," as he referred to his mission) that he had begun. Paul's sense of timing and fulfillment overrides any concerns for his personal safety.

This begs questions about prophecies and prophets, Theophilus, which I will not touch upon here. I doubt whether anyone around us at the time could have intervened and convinced Paul otherwise. We were simply not at his level of authority and were ourselves still learning what it meant to be "overseers" or "co-workers." Even Agabus, a well-tested oracular voice from Jerusalem, was overruled.

> Acts 21:3–7 **3** We came in sight of Cyprus; and leaving it on our left, we sailed to Syria and landed at Tyre, because the ship was to unload its cargo there. **4** We looked up the disciples and stayed there for seven days. Through the Spirit they told Paul not to go on to Jerusalem. **5** When our days there were ended, we left and proceeded on our journey; and all of them, with wives and children, escorted us outside the city. There we knelt down on the beach and prayed **6** and said farewell to one another. Then we went on board the ship, and they returned home. **7** When we had finished the voyage from Tyre, we arrived at Ptolemais; and we greeted the believers and stayed with them for one day.

> Acts 21:8–10 **8** On the morrow we departed and came to Caesarea; and we entered the house of Philip the evangelist, who was one of the seven, and stayed with him. **9** And he had four unmarried daughters, who prophesied. **10** While we were staying for some days, a prophet named Agabus came down from Judea.

1. Have I ever seen prophecy at work in a church setting? How? Is there a role for prophecy or supernatural guidance in my life or in the group I am part of?

2. Could Paul have avoided the perils that lay before him? Are there clues in the narrative up to this point that Paul is doing the right thing? Search into the commission Paul was given when he first met the prophet Ananias.

3. Are there times when it feels that I cannot or should not stop the flow of things that lie before me, even when it brings me into perils? How should one be strong in such circumstances?

# The Catechumenate in the Temple

On the other hand, Jerusalem did present a core of leaders who could and would address Paul's fundamental choices about mission and life. After all, some of them bore the mantle of "Apostle" because Jesus had directly summoned them, while Paul could only claim such status indirectly by way of vision. Paul consistently recognized their oversight of his work during all these years of travels. Among them still stood the very James who had issued the Apostolic Decree affirming Paul's efforts to bring Jew and Gentile together. Even if the full repercussions of that ruling were still unfolding (and often misunderstood), it was James who presided over the general Church acceptance of the policy. It was this Decree that was inextricably tied to Paul and the controversy surrounding his cooperative work among Jews and Gentiles.

After hearing him out, the leaders at Jerusalem asked Paul to profile himself as an observant and devout Jew. This would counter the negative reputation that dogged him everywhere he went, and especially here among the Judeans. He agreed to commit himself to yet another vow that he would fulfill in the temple in the presence of all his critics.

Here, let me explain a bit of what this vow would do for him. First, he had to show that he supported the separation between Jew and Gentile on some level by "cleansing" himself of anything foreign that prevented entrance into the restricted area of the temple. The process of keeping a vow began with such a symbolic act. Second, if he followed through on this vow, James and the others felt he would pacify those who believed that Paul stood for wiping out ethnic distinctions—for only devout Jews put themselves under such strictures.

Although Paul knew that even this action could be misinterpreted or disparaged by his opponents, he felt it did not violate his conscience (after all he done it before) and might be a public relations coup. As in Ephesus, the disinformation machine continued to antagonize Paul's best efforts. By now, his opponents had a veritable "catechumenate" machine set up in Jerusalem, and it pumped out disinformation about Paul by the barrel. When I wrote you my narrative earlier, I used the same word to describe their propaganda as what I said about catechumenizing Apollos. Paul, in consultation with the Council, agreed to confront that negative image with his own public testimony. Just as at Ephesus, this effort in Jerusalem would ultimately fail.

Acts 21:20–22 **20**When they heard it, they praised God. Then they said to him, "You see, brother, how many thousands of believers there are among the Jews, and they are all zealous for the law. **21** They have been told about you that you teach all the Jews living among the Gentiles to forsake Moses, and that you tell them not to circumcise their children or observe the customs. **22** What then is to be done? They will certainly hear that you have come."

Acts 21:23–24 **23**"Do therefore what we tell you. We have four men who are under a vow; **24** take these men and purify yourself along with them and pay their expenses, so that they may shave their heads. Thus all will know that there is nothing in what they have been told about you but that you yourself live in observance of the law."

1. Do I have peers that can speak into my life? Do I allow such folks to have access to my decision-making?

2. How can I go about finding those to whom I can be accountable?

3. Does Paul's carrying out a "vow" seem phony? How important is "public relations" to me?

## In the Nick of Time

I don't think any of the Council recognized how vitriolic Paul's opposition was. Because of Paul's farewells in various places between Macedonia and Judea, his return was certainly no secret to anyone. He had deliberately plodded along because he wanted to savor this last "pilgrimage" to Jerusalem—whatever the outcome, prison or Rome, so these times would probably be the last times he would see their faces. Nonetheless, his arrival was anticipated and parsed by critics in the most hostile fashion. It did not help of course that Paul had his entourage with him wherever he went in the city, and it included Gentiles who were prohibited from entering sacred space in the temple.

So James's strategy of trying to win over the Judean zealots actually backfired in the face of an unruly temple crowd. My earlier account to you implied that instead of 'catechizing' those who were ignorant, the appearance of Paul in the temple caused them "confusion"—the Greek antonym of the first term. The whole scene became reminiscent of Paul at the Temple of Artemis, where clients of Demetrius turned things into a public melee. Where Paul's reputation threatened the business clientele in Ephesus, here he threatened the religious lobby.

The final point to observe is that the antidote to the earlier riot is the same here: the forces of law and order come to Paul's aid in the nick of time. Where Ephesus has Asiarchs who befriended Paul and the city clerk who urged calm and order, here there are the tribune and his troops. In both cases, the civil authorities save Paul and ultimately contribute to a strategy that requires patience and finesse.

> Acts 21:27–30 **27** When the seven days were almost completed, the Jews from Asia, who had seen him in the temple, stirred up the whole crowd. They seized him, **28** shouting, "Fellow Israelites, help! This is the man who is teaching everyone everywhere against our people, our law, and this place; more than that, he has actually brought Greeks into the temple and has defiled this holy place." **29** For they had previously seen Trophimus the Ephesian with him in the city, and they supposed that Paul had brought him into the temple. **30** Then all the city was aroused, and the people rushed together. They seized Paul and dragged him out of the temple, and immediately the doors were shut.

> Acts 21:31–39 **31** And as they were trying to kill him, word came to the tribune of the cohort that all Jerusalem was in confusion. **32** He at once took soldiers and centurions, and ran down to them; and when they saw the tribune and the soldiers, they stopped beating Paul. **33** Then the tribune came up and arrested him, and ordered him to be bound with two chains. He inquired who he was and what he had done. **34** Some in the crowd shouted one thing, some another; and as he could not learn the facts because of the uproar, he ordered him to be brought into the barracks. **35** And when he came to the steps, he was actually carried by the soldiers because of the violence of the crowd; **36** for the mob of the people followed, crying, "Away with him!" **37** As Paul was about to be brought into the barracks, he said to the tribune, "May I say something to you?" And he said, "Do you know Greek? **38** Are you not the Egyptian, then, who recently stirred up a revolt and led the four thousand men of the Assassins out into the wilderness?" **39** Paul replied, "I am a Jew, from Tarsus in Cilicia, a citizen of no mean city; I beg you, let me speak to the people."

1. Can I remember times when I have been rescued in the nick of time? Was it a matter of vindication for me?

2. Have there been times when the more I tried to explain myself, the more I failed to clarify things? How about times when the more I tried to rectify matter, the more things fell apart? How did I react? How would I react today?

3. Take time to consider places where the Gospel has been protected by secular authorities, and pray for renewed or continuing security for those who are threatened.

# Chapter 22

## Apologia

Obtaining one last opportunity to address the Jerusalem masses, Paul gives his public apologia. While the reports of Paul's defense in various places do not match in every detail, this speech does emphasize points by which I am sure Paul meant to pacify his audience.

For one thing, he takes pains to tell them he understands their ardent desire for perfection and devotion. He uses himself as example, citing his own passion and then a reversal of conviction. Sometimes, he implies, such desire can turn so intransigent that it can only be penetrated by direct and divine intervention. Zeal without divine light is perhaps not immoral, but it is blind.

Thus you will notice that Paul never seemed to show shame whenever he confessed his life's earlier zeal and impeccable consistency. Indeed, the very next day before the Sanhedrin he would testify to a clear conscience throughout his life no matter how complicit he was in the death of Stephen. He was completely wrong, yes, but only because of blindness.

That is why "scales" had to fall from his eyes, and in some sense he sees these same scales upon the eyes of his audience. Theophilus, you need to realize that for Paul and his zealous confreres, religion is no passing fad. They are militant about observing their religion, and militants require enormous intervention to change.So Paul identifies with his audience by telling them about his own misguided zeal.

He also tells them—and it was the first time I heard this—that shortly after his conversion, he had yet another personal encounter with Jesus, who encouraged and commissioned him. First, he laid out a future for Paul away from Jerusalem and foretold the slander that would rise against him because of his unswerving allegiance.

Second, Jesus assured Paul that he would make a path for him leading to a whole new mission. It is this mission that his ethnic peers revile because it implies that Paul is on the side of the Gentiles. Already the Asian pilgrims have noticed Trophimus the Ephesian in Jerusalem, and they assume he has ventured into space forbidden to outsiders. This issue of including the Gentiles had trailed Paul ever since the Apostolic Decree. Paul had touched a raw nerve when he so easily reached out to Gentiles and thus any mention of what he did in this regard easily ignited Judean zealots. Paul had tried the empathetic approach, recounting his own antagonism toward the Way, but this time the scales did not fall off the eyes of his listeners.

When things were spinning out of control once again, Paul claimed full force of law to protect himself. This time he asserted his birthright Roman citizenship, and it obtained instant results. The tribune immediately exercised every imperial right and privilege to protect Paul.

> Acts 22:3–5 **3** "I am a Jew, born in Tarsus in Cilicia, but brought up in this city at the feet of Gamaliel, educated strictly according to our ancestral law, being zealous for God, just as all of you are today. **4** I persecuted this Way up to the point of death by binding both men and women and putting them in prison, **5** as the high priest and the whole council of elders can testify about me. From them I also received letters to the brothers in Damascus, and I went there in order to bind those who were there and to bring them back to Jerusalem for punishment."

> Acts 22:17–21 **17** "After I had returned to Jerusalem and while I was praying in the temple, I fell into a trance **18** and saw Jesus saying to me, 'Hurry and get out of Jerusalem quickly, because they will not accept your testimony about me.' **19** And I said, 'Lord, they themselves know that in every synagogue I imprisoned and beat those who believed in you. **20** And while the blood of your witness Stephen was shed, I myself was standing by, approving and keeping the coats of those who killed him.' **21** Then he said to me, 'Go, for I will send you far away to the Gentiles.'"

> Acts 22:28–29 **28** The tribune answered, "I bought this citizenship for a large sum." Paul said, "But I was born a citizen." **29** So those who were about to examine him withdrew from him instantly; and the tribune also was afraid, for he realized that Paul was a Roman citizen and that he had bound him.

1. When have I ever been so convinced about my correctness that only a stroke from the blue convinced me otherwise? Was I to blame in my certitude, or just completely mistaken?

2. How is faith like scales removed from our eyes? Have I ever prayed for those who are completely and seemingly genuinely convinced that faith is bogus or simply impossible?

3. What strategies have I used to win over those who disagree with me? Has empathy worked? Has it not worked at times? Have I tried it with those who disagree with me on matters of faith?

## Letting Go of Jerusalem

The Almighty often intervened in Paul's life in the flow of ministry and not in the stillness of contemplation. For Paul would set out in one direction with kinetic energy, only to find himself channeled elsewhere. Take, for example, his initial desire to make Asia Minor and its vast inland territory the scope of his travels only to learn that he should go to Macedonia. Or when he seemed like he had failed yet again in Corinth and was ready to give up there: only a divine visitation could keep him in place—and remarkably he stayed for another eighteen months.

The fierce encounters with the rank and file and leadership in Jerusalem once again forced him to reevaluate everything. For much of his third missionary journey, an inner eye seemed to keep him transfixed on some intangible climax. Paul imagined it to be a last hurrah in Jerusalem, and so he busily worked to consolidate what he began at the four corners of his travels. Then, at the end of his preparations, he bid farewell to all the churches he had founded and to all the workers he trained.

He had steeled himself for Jerusalem, and even divinely appointed prophets could not dissuade him from his end goal. This, he thought, would be the fulfillment of the course laid out for him when he first received his commission from Jesus himself—and Jerusalem was appropriate for someone as dedicated to his traditions as Paul.

So it was a real shocker when another revelation now came to Paul. The Lord came and stood by him, almost to brace him for the news: His current afflictions would only be a prelude to Paul's next phase of the mission in Rome and not Jerusalem!

What would have happened had not Paul received these mysterious interventions in the course of his life? Would he have continued in Asia? Would he have given up in Corinth? In this case, would he have simply followed through in his resolution to die in Jerusalem in spite of all the warning he received? Instead, he now sought to do everything in his power now to stay alive, to alert the tribune about the plot against him and to press on with his Roman rights for a trial before Caesar. In this moment, he must have felt a surge of grace to continue on with his resistance until he would stand in Rome, probably clueless about what an enormous cost would be exacted for fulfilling the divine plan.

Paul had been oriented toward Jerusalem throughout his life. After all, he had originally moved here from abroad precisely because of his ethnic and religious loyalties. Even after the scales fell from his eyes, he kept Jerusalem in view: his constant return to Jerusalem to visit the apostolic representatives, his collection of the alms from diaspora groups, his resolve to return to Jerusalem to report to the Apostolic Council, his hastening to Jerusalem by Pentecost. Yet because of this new revelation that he must bear witness in Rome, he gave up his lifelong dream to go back—to live and die in Jerusalem—and astonishingly embraced a new destination. Paul had earlier expressed an interest in visiting Rome, but he had never imagined it would be under these circumstances. Now he realized that finishing the course would mean not only saying farewell to Asia Minor, Macedonia, and Greece, but giving up Jerusalem as his final resting place.

## Paul's Lamentation

Stones and walls of Jerusalem,
Tracing your tattoos on my heart,
Would I so quick leave you ungrieved
To gain Caesar and Rome as my part?

Jerusalem, early I loved you,
When soul was aflame in my youth;
Steered clear for you of marriage bond,
Lusting for your form and couth.

O city fathers, O city sons,
To you pledged I as virgin bride!

My soul was trothed to take none else
As my love, my joy, my pride.

How many years I nursed my dream
Let Jerusalem's souks be filled!
All at once will I lose your charm,
Those songs and feasts that often thrilled?

Far from you I go, O land of my dreams,
Forced now to go elsewhere by spite.
Years have I spent to earn thee as prize.
With wormwood and gall do you requite?

You spurned, but would I reject
What kin has entitled me as heir?
You hunted as prey and viewed me as foe,
And left me but tears as my share.

How many years did I cheer your future,
With Jerusalem as my glory and lens?
Then Jesus stretched out to crown all my zeal
To comfort with hearty amends.

He too was spurned, while speaking to you,
Of true Zion—not stones and walls.
He who met me could not but let me
Be guide for the Gentiles he calls.

Once trod I these steps of Israel's tribes,
With Jerusalem, here and now, my goal.
Now lately you come, to whisper this truth:
Move on to Rome, O my soul!


Acts 23:11 The following night the Lord stood by him and said,
"Take courage, for as you have testified about me at Jerusalem, so
you must bear witness also at Rome."

1. Have I ever had to give up a long-held goal or aspiration? How difficult was it? What eventually helped to overcome my disappointment?

2. How has God helped me to find another way, when I knew that my best efforts had failed?

Fig. 9: *Paul Leaves Jerusalem*, by Jamie Treadwell.
Used with the permission of the artist.

# Chapter 23

## Pulling Strings

Though Paul realized that his hopes and dreams for Jerusalem could not measure up to the grim realities on the ground, he managed to tap into a network of connections to keep himself alive. His family had settled here many years earlier, so his nephew picked up wind of a deadly plot the Judean zealots fomented against him. His birthright credentials as a citizen give him relative comforts and access even though he is an imperial prisoner of the Roman legionaries. This allows Paul's nephew to visit Paul and let him know about the conspiracy. Paul is able to summon and press a centurion to bring the lad's information to the tribune. Now that is pulling strings!

Roman protection immediately is granted Paul, and conspicuous aid at that: one quarter of the detachment's total force is dispatched for Paul's safety and for his subsequent travel to Caesarea—where even larger and more self-standing Roman forces are based. His status means that he will face no indigenous threat to his life and welfare.

The irony of it all—and I am tempted to call it "divinely instigated" irony—is that Paul will depend on such Roman security to make it all the way from Jerusalem to Rome. Further, he depends on an imperial letter (from the tribune) to establish his integrity before the Roman governor of Palestine, who will then pass on its claims to other imperial authorities along the way. The letter specifically assures one and all that the tribune had found "nothing deserving of death or imprisonment." Once Paul arrives, he makes use of the fact that he was born in Cilicia, where Rome would have even more jurisdiction than in Jerusalem. Paul quickly sizes up what is required for passage and pulls every string. Now he is not merely a Jew, bound by spiritual gravity for Jerusalem; now he is a delegate of Maker of heaven and earth, a Roman citizen bound for the city to which all roads lead. I wonder, Theophilus, if I hear faint echoes of that divine laughter that goes way back to the first time the Church encountered "the rage of the kings of the earth and rulers against the Lord and his anointed."

> Acts 23:23–35  **23** Then he called two of the centurions and said, "At the third hour of the night get ready two hundred soldiers with seventy horsemen and two hundred spearmen to go as far as Caesarea. **24** Also provide mounts for Paul to ride, and bring him safely to Felix the governor." **25** And he wrote a letter to this effect: **26** "Claudius Lysias to his Excellency the governor Felix, greeting. **27** This man was seized by the Jews, and was about to be killed by them, when I came upon them with the soldiers and rescued him, having learned that he was a Roman citizen. **28** And desiring to know the charge on which they accused him, I brought him down to their council. **29** I found that he was accused about questions of their law, but charged with nothing deserving death or imprisonment. **30** And when it was disclosed to me that there would be a plot against the man, I sent him to you at once, ordering his accusers also to state before you what they have against him." **31** So the soldiers, according to their instructions, took Paul and brought him by night to Antipatris. **32** And on the morrow they returned to the barracks, leaving the horsemen to go on with him. **33** When they came to Caesarea and delivered the letter to the governor, they presented Paul also before him. **34** On reading the letter, he asked to what province he belonged. When he learned that he was from Cilicia **35** he said, "I will hear you when your accusers arrive." And he commanded him to be guarded in Herod's praetorium.

1. Have I ever pulled strings to ensure the success of things I am concerned about? Give some examples.

2. What is the relationship between worldly and divine authority in this passage? Is it at work in the world today, awares or unawares?

3. Are there any other divine "ironies" of history or of my life, where I know how things will fall into place or where I can say that the Almighty has made things happen? What lessons can I learn from these examples?

# On Trial

When the attorneys get involved, you know that it is time to take off the gloves in the boxing arena. Whereas before Paul rarely collided with Caesar's delegates, now he is standing trial at the governor's bench and has to defend himself before formal litigators. The Judeans knew that they could not reach into that Roman world with their idiosyncratic and sometimes clandestine procedures, so they have to go public with their suit against Paul. They hired an attorney, a good one, who knew how to butter up the Roman governor as well as lay out a case that would be incriminating. The case their prosecutor, Tertullus, laid out seemed to me convincing—or at least he convinced me that almost every charge he made was true.

Paul was unfazed by Tertullus. He rose in his own defense and eloquently refuted everything. Paul never ceases to amaze me: he could debate philosophers in Athens using their own poetry and arguments, and now he waxes eloquent with imperial etiquette, classical rhetoric, and Roman law! Somehow he managed to turn the tables on their attorney's charges, suggesting that they lacked the burden of proof. We all knew that he had won a knockout when he made his legal defense a bully pulpit for theological persuasion. Not only did he win a reprieve from their prosecution, but was granted continued good accommodations from the governor himself.

Paul says that he has acted with "a clear conscience," meaning that he has maintained integrity in his personal dealings and would withstand scrutiny. This equally applies to Paul when he faced the Sanhedrin and faced the Asian Jews who accused him in the temple. Moreover, Paul has maintained this integrity throughout his missionary enterprise; and he testifies to it when he addresses the topic of his involvement among the Ephesian elders and as he speaks to the Jewish mob. The fact of the matter, as I stated above, is that it even held for when he persecuted believers! This is truly a robust conscience—one that I have not often run into among his fellow Israelites.

> Acts 24:1–8 **1**Five days later the high priest Ananias came down with some elders and an attorney, a certain Tertullus, and they reported their case against Paul to the governor. **2** When Paul had been summoned, Tertullus began to accuse him, saying: "Your Excellency, because of you we have long enjoyed peace, and reforms have been made for this people because of your foresight. **3** We welcome this in every way and everywhere with utmost gratitude. **4** But, to detain you no further, I beg you to hear us briefly with

your customary graciousness. **5** We have, in fact, found this man a pestilent fellow, an agitator among all the Jews throughout the world, and a ringleader of the sect of the Nazarenes. **6** He even tried to profane the temple, and so we seized him. **7** **8** By examining him yourself you will be able to learn from him concerning everything of which we accuse him."

Acts 24:11–14 **11** "As you can find out, it is not more than twelve days since I went up to worship in Jerusalem. **12** They did not find me disputing with anyone in the temple or stirring up a crowd either in the synagogues or throughout the city. **13** Neither can they prove to you the charge that they now bring against me. **14** But this I admit to you, that according to the Way, which they call a sect, I worship the God of our ancestors, believing everything laid down according to the law or written in the prophets."

Acts 24:16 "So I always take pains to have a clear conscience toward God and toward men."

1. Imagine what I would do if implicated in a lawsuit or prosecuted in criminal court. How would I defend myself?

2. What is my state of conscience? Is it "robust" enough to stave off false accusations of guilt? Do I easily capitulate when attacked in character?

## Languishing

The imperial government is a buffer against persecution and vigilantes, yes, but Paul now runs into its apparent stubborn resistance to the divine plan: I mean, if Rome is his appointed objective, why do the Roman authorities now seem to stand in the way? The governor who presided over his trial would hardly be Paul's choice for case adjudicator: his name was Felix, and his sultry and scandalous reputation preceded him. He claimed to know a lot about the "Way" that Paul represented. His beautiful Jewish wife, no matter how rumor had it that he won her, probably kept him posted on the reports surrounding Jesus and his followers.

Whatever the facts surrounding his character, Felix was willing to look to Paul's comforts, but lacked the will to release him. He could exhibit moments of conscience, like when he and his Jewish wife privately consulted with Paul and inquired about his faith in Jesus. Being an educated Roman, he might have been as intrigued as the philosophers at Athens about such questions as "justice and self-control and future judgment." The question, though, is whether he granted access for Paul to speak to his soul's inner agitation and restlessness.

When all is said and done, he offered nothing to Paul and the Kingdom beyond what his tawdry life presaged. For he was a corrupt and greedy politician who could not bring himself to do the right thing. Being an obsequious bureaucrat who connived his way to a high political position, he could not take a step in the direction of courage. No wonder he let Paul languish in his custody for two years without resolution. No wonder his fascination with Paul was punctuated with worries whenever the topic about "justice and self-control and future judgment" arose. In short, Felix was hardly the herald of what his name in Latin, "blessed one," announced.

And Paul knew it. Paul must have seen a pygmy of a man in front of him, entrusted with far more responsibility than his character could bear. Felix's instincts were trained to seek out political favor in public and financial gain in private. What doubts must have come to Paul when he imagined that his fate rested in the hands of this man, a man who had one ear on Paul's sermons, the other on the Judean politics in Jerusalem! Double-mindedness founds its Platonic ideal in Felix . . .

Meanwhile, Paul waits for vindication. After the Lord had so long ago stood by him when he had given up his dreams of Jerusalem and assured him that he would testify in Rome, still he sits here languishing in prison. What would he have uttered, had I been able to interview him? 'Valuable time lost?' 'Did I really experience the divine presence? Why this delay?' 'What makes me so sure that I will fulfill the course as I imagined it?'

Even Paul's normally poignant polemics about the Kingdom sputters out in the presence of this half-hearted and double-minded politician. How often our testimony falls on deaf ears or fails to reverberate with faith among those who are not converted! We may work diligently to present the gospel without results—and fruitlessness always leaves us frustrated. I can only believe, Theophilus, that Paul had something he would not let go, no matter what the current circumstances communicated. Paul had learned over the years not to pay attention to what the harbingers of gloom predicted.

## Epigram: A Riddle

So, Felix, I riddle to you
As before to Eutychus, your twin:
Do you bear your name lightly?
Will you find your luck again?
Your twin asleep while listening,
Fell dead upon the ground.
Will you, dead to Paul's word,
Now awake to its sound?
One, fortunate to be alive;
Felix, alive to find fortune.
Will both of you dither and stall?
Will both of you miss your call?

## Epigram: Mute

Paul, keep you vigil always
In the night or in the jail?
Forever, Paul, in the dark?
Or now your hope prevail?
By night, you raised a boy to life;
Now Felix calls you from your cell:
Will either stir and turn their heart
To find their heaven or hell?
Paul, you stay in darkness mute
Through two years you nary speak.
Will you grit your teeth for long?
Or will you abide so meek?

Acts 24:24–27 **24** After some days Felix came with his wife Drusilla, who was a Jewess; and he sent for Paul and heard him speak upon faith in Christ Jesus. **25** And as he argued about justice and self-control and future judgment, Felix was alarmed and said, "Go away for the present; when I have an opportunity I will summon you." **26** At the same time he hoped that money would be given him by Paul. So he sent for him often and conversed with him.

**27** But when two years had elapsed, Felix was succeeded by Porcius Festus; and desiring to do the Jews a favor, Felix left Paul in prison.

1.  What would be my reaction to systematic or bureaucratic obstacles to something I ardently support? How do I deal with people who are resisting what I advocate?

2.  How well am I currently holding on to my God-given dream or vision in the face of apparent contradiction or defeat?

3.  What am I prepared to sacrifice or endure to stay faithful to my calling?

4.  Who are some of the persons I have tried to reach for a long time without success? How persistent am I in sharing the gospel when it seems to make no headway?

# Chapter 24

## Habeas Corpus

Yet, in the face of this corrupt and two-faced governor-judge Felix, Paul somehow would overcome all obstacles and make his way to Rome. Somehow Paul mustered the internal assurance to endure and to prevail. He outlasted Felix's schemes without compromising himself. And then he proactively seized the moment when the next imperial governor, Festus, gave him a hearing: he demanded that he receive his legal privileges as a Roman citizen to face his accusers and to make an appeal to Caesar.

Speaking in his own defense, Paul knows his rights and exercises them. The logical way out would have been to go to Jerusalem, but the revelation that Paul received in his jail cell that he would go to Rome made him decline this offer. In every review of the facts surrounding the Jews' case against Paul, it was clear he would be exonerated. You would be hard-pressed to find anyone not caught up in the machinations of the Jerusalem elites who would have found Paul guilty of anything. Even the likes of Felix recognized this.

As you know, Theophilus, originally Paul felt so strongly that he should go to Jerusalem that he was willing to be imprisoned and to die there. This outcome had already been envisioned by Paul when dire warnings accompanied him on his final journey to the holy city. Agabus, for example, a well-known prophet whose predictions had been accurate in the past, came down from Jerusalem to tell him about what would happen if he continued on his way. For all of the drama of that prophecy—Agabus bound himself up with Paul's belt—Paul seemed to miss the second part of Agabus's words: "the Jews will bind . . . and deliver [Paul] into the hands of the Gentiles." Paul had interpreted it as a call to be ready to die in Jerusalem.

It was only later that the Lord stood by him in his jail cell and clarified that he would go to Rome. This inner conviction must have been what made him go to such lengths to defend himself and to appeal all the way to the emperor, for he would now embrace this God-given destiny.

Imagine what the power of that revelation was to Paul. It empowered him to make his defense before Felix and later Festus and Agrippa and the whole imperial and royal entourage of Caesarea. On the rational level, everyone was convinced he would be set free if he had agreed to Festus's terms of a trial in Jerusalem. On an emotional level, Paul was already willing to die in Jerusalem, perhaps because he had envisioned for himself a fate like Jesus or the prophets. For it was common belief that prophets and holy men met their fate in Jerusalem. Yet as so often in his life, Paul makes unprecedented and unexpected decisions and proceeds in directions that are direct responses to divine revelations.

Two other points are worth noting, Theophilus, as long as we are re-evaluating Paul's reaction to the legal process in this unfinished tale:

1. Paul is not afraid of testifying before the highest authorities—he acts as his own attorney. He reminds me of a passage I often read growing up, "I will speak of your testimony before kings and shall not be put to shame; for I find my delight in your statutes which I love; and I swear by your statutes, which I love."[1] Paul is fighting big forces here: the institutional authorities, the political government that wishes to appease its local clients, and the religious elites that want to maintain its grasp of power; but he holds his head high and acts as his own attorney. If earlier he spoke directly against the corruptions of Felix by speaking about "righteousness and self-control and the coming judgment," here he speaks brazenly of his rights to appeal to Caesar—and this in front of an assembly of the leading men in all their regalia. But he does not wilt before his scrutinizers, and he does not fail to act assertively and persuasively.

2. On a side note: Paul does not dispute the death penalty's correctness. If he has done something so seriously wrong that deserves death, he does not gainsay its correctness as a measure that the state can exercise. His dispute is not with the Empire but with the charges raised against him.

---

1. Ps 119:46–47.

Acts 25:8–12  **8** Paul said in his defense, "Neither against the law of the Jews, nor against the temple, nor against Caesar have I offended at all." **9** But Festus, wishing to do the Jews a favor, said to Paul, "Do you wish to go up to Jerusalem, and there be tried on these charges before me?" **10** But Paul said, "I am standing before Caesar's tribunal, where I ought to be tried; to the Jews I have done no wrong, as you know very well. **11** If then I am a wrongdoer, and have committed anything for which I deserve to die, I do not seek to escape death; but if there is nothing in their charges against me, no one can give me up to them. I appeal to Caesar." **12** Then Festus, when he had conferred with his council, answered, "You have appealed to Caesar; to Caesar you shall go."

Acts 25:23–27  **23** So on the morrow Agrippa and Bernice came with great pomp, and they entered the audience hall with the military tribunes and the prominent men of the city. Then by command of Festus Paul was brought in. **24** And Festus said, "King Agrippa and all who are present with us, you see this man about whom the whole Jewish people petitioned me, both at Jerusalem and here, shouting that he ought not to live any longer. **25** But I found that he had done nothing deserving death; and as he himself appealed to the emperor, I decided to send him. **26** But I have nothing definite to write to my lord about him. Therefore I have brought him before you, and, especially before you, King Agrippa, that, after we have examined him, I may have something to write. **27** For it seems to me unreasonable, in sending a prisoner, not to indicate the charges against him."

1. Have I ever made a high-stakes gamble when I could have settled secure for something much less? Did I win? What did I lose? In retrospect, did I make the right decision?

2. Have I ever faced a public evaluation or scrutiny? What did it feel like? How much courage did it take?

3. Now try to put yourself in Paul's place and imagine the pressure on him. Describe it. What resources would I draw on to endure?

# Chapter 25

## Two-Minute Testimony

When Paul says that he is "fortunate," the word here [26:2] *makarios* (μακάριος) a word that most often is connected with bliss or blessedness. Earlier, Paul said he would make his defense "cheerfully" (εὐθύμως, *euthymōs* [24:10]) when he spoke to Felix; but here he is more than cheerful. Cheerfulness is a choice or posture the steadfast man takes, but blessedness is bestowed upon the steadfast man, as something like a reward. Why does Paul use this term in these circumstances? Because he is addressing an initiated audience—that is, they are like a class that has already done their homework and are now ready for the lesson. They know that blessedness is a commendation from God for a deed well done.

Agrippa is an observant Jew. Thus, Paul knows he can speak of "customs and controversies of the Jews" and because he suspects that Agrippa is already piously aware of the "hope" and the "prophets" that the people of Israel hold. Paul launches into a disquisition full of presuppositions. And it all must have registered with his audience, for at one point Paul exclaims, "I know that you believe" what I am talking about.

In effect, Paul realizes that he has about two-minutes of floor time to make his case, and he seizes the moment. His statements are chock-full and dense with information not reported in his earlier defenses. He skips events and intermediaries to get to his main point. What is his main point? It is found in his two-fold mission statement:

1. Look at my original text if you have it there [v. 16]: Paul says he is first a servant and a witness, that is, he is supposed to be like a table waiter and serve the meal to the Lord's guests and he is also an observer of what the Lord has done and what the Lord will do. In other words, this

testimony is not Paul's initiative, but God's. Primarily, Paul has seen the Lord at work already, and he must bear witness to those things. Beyond those previous things, he is also supposed to testify to those things the Lord will show him. In my account, you have already seen how Paul has executed this commission as he responds to the Lord's revelations, for example, the revelation to bring the gospel to Macedonia, the decision to stay in Corinth for a long period, and (even now) the decision to appeal to Caesar.

2. Then the next part [v. 17]. There are two components to his job definition: first to convert his listeners ("to open their eyes"), and second to make them disciples ("that they may turn from darkness to light," and from "the power of Satan to God"). This dual purpose is repeated in the last clause: "that they may receive forgiveness of sins" (first step of conversion) and "a place among those who are sanctified by faith" (discipleship). "Repent and turn" are the two things Paul is supposed to offer and witness in his mission, and they encompass what walking along the Way means.

These things Paul will do for anyone who is ready, both "small and great." We have seen, Theophilus, the ones Paul has in mind: those like Lydia of Philippi and the Asiarch Roman citizens in Ephesus, the tribune in Jerusalem and the consul in Corinth, the governor in Jerusalem, Dionysius at the Areopagus, anyone and everyone, high and low, rich and poor. He will do it now for Agrippa and Bernice and soon for Caesar, Jew and Gentile. Thus, Paul's work is interracial, intercultural, and cuts across all classes of people.

When all is said and done in this compact message to Agrippa, the king notices that Paul's aim is to convert and disciple him in a "short order," that is, in the two minutes he has been talking. Of course, the short time Paul speaks is not the unit by which God will measure its power or impact. You have heard it said, "A thousand years in God's sight is like a day already gone by or as a vigil in the night."[1] What we have seen throughout this narrative is that flashes of insight and revelation often play out in months or years: when God stood beside Paul in jail two years earlier and gave assurance, the actual fulfillment would take its time and toil and toll. We don't see the outcome of Paul's testimony here, but Paul's life cries out to us that some initiatives take a long time and some a short time.

1. Ps 90:4.

The length of time does not deter Paul as he "cheerfully" has given his apologias in the past and now here "blissfully" testifies to royal dignitaries. I don't know how Paul stood so adamantly under such duress, but he never flinched as long as I knew him. The stresses would not stop, but neither would Paul's inner light and irrepressible joy.

The only pangs I noticed here in this particular trial was his anguish that his listeners become converted and change. The hearing ended in embarrassed recognition that Paul's fate was no longer in the hands of Paul's enemies or the distinguished audience before him now. It was not even in Paul's hands: now even King Agrippa was struck by Paul's testimony and sensed that the divine plan had overridden every effort to the contrary. It was the stroke of One who sits in the heavens, the one who laughs last.

> Acts 26:2–3 **2** "I think myself fortunate that it is before you, King Agrippa, I am to make my defense today against all the accusations of the Jews, **3** because you are especially familiar with all customs and controversies of the Jews; therefore I beg you to listen to me patiently."

> Acts 26:14–18 **14** "And when we had all fallen to the ground, I heard a voice saying to me in the Hebrew language, 'Saul, Saul, why do you persecute me? It hurts you to kick against the goads.' **15** And I said, 'Who are you, Lord?' And the Lord said, 'I am Jesus whom you are persecuting. **16** But rise and stand upon your feet; for I have appeared to you for this purpose, to appoint you to serve and bear witness to the things in which you have seen me and to those in which I will appear to you, **17** delivering you from the people and from the Gentiles—to whom I send you **18** to open their eyes, that they may turn from darkness to light and from the power of Satan to God, that they may receive forgiveness of sins and a place among those who are sanctified by faith in me.'"

> Acts 26:27–29 **27** "King Agrippa, do you believe the prophets? I know that you believe." **28** And Agrippa said to Paul, "In a short time you think to make me a Christian!" **29** And Paul said, "Whether short or long, I would to God that not only you but also all who hear me this day might become such as I am—except for these chains."

1. What would I say if I were to give a two-minute justification for my life? How does my "testimony" resonate with faith? Have I ever had opportunities to share my life-story in a brief period of time?

2. As Paul stands in chains, he says he is "blessed." Why does he say this?

3. Consider what situations I have been in when, even though I am shackled by circumstances, I can say I am "blessed." How did I relate to these situations at the time?

## Providence?

Paul is dispatched to Rome, a ship bearing him prisoner to Caesar, much like my story takes you, Theophilus, to its end. What is the lesson we learn as our ships near their destination? Remarkably Paul is allowed the companionship of friends like Aristarchus and me. So, I suppose, this shows that his final speech in Caesarea had achieved some kind of sympathetic response from his audience. The guard assigned him was a centurion from an elite military corps assigned to Palestine, thus, a man who had connections with imperial officials along the way to Rome.

Even more remarkable is the fact that this highly placed imperial guard is philanthropic in his attentiveness to Paul's needs. Again this strikes me as a nod toward Paul's effectiveness before Festus and Agrippa. This soldier, whose name is Julius, allows Aristarchus and me to come aboard as Paul's friends even though our presence would have pricked the nerves of the Judeans who want nothing less than an ignominious elimination of the Way. Contrary to their designs, Julius will increasingly pay attention to Paul and value his advice, even though he is dealing with a boatload of Rome's alleged enemies.

Following the calendar since Paul made that fateful decision to return to Jerusalem, it seems that the days turn into weeks and then into years, and even now the boat ever so slowly makes its way up the Asian coast before it turns west toward its destination. Paul initially wanted to return to Jerusalem for the Day of Atonement, and had hoped that he could burnish his credentials as a true son of Israel by announcing a religious vow. Since then he had been arrested, tried without verdict, and incarcerated for two years. It had thrown off the religious calendar he had so assiduously followed over the years as an observant Jew. To a casual observer, it seemed that Paul was a prisoner to randomness as much as to Rome.

Further, it seemed that even the natural flow of time—the very seasons of summer and winter—conspire to thwart what we all had imagined as our story's end. Nonetheless, if the authorities that governed religion and politics could not thwart Paul's final destiny and destination, neither can the seas and winds withstand the divine providence. But take heed, Theophilus: Providence is triggered by Paul's pluck and wiliness, and a host of "coincidences." Everything will weave together so as to fulfill the revelation made so long ago in Paul's prison cell. It is a sovereign hand at work, deriding—or at least wryly overriding all obstacles.

> Acts 27:1–3  ¹And when it was decided that we should sail for Italy, they delivered Paul and some other prisoners to a centurion of the Augustan Cohort, named Julius. ² And embarking in a ship of Adramyttium, which was about to sail to the ports along the coast of Asia, we put to sea, accompanied by Aristarchus, a Macedonian from Thessalonica. ³ The next day we put in at Sidon; and Julius treated Paul kindly, and gave him leave to go to his friends and be cared for.

1. Have I ever experienced how a sponsor or mentor looked out for me and kept me from getting into trouble? Am I returning this grace by looking after someone given to me to help?

2. What is the relationship between divine providence and human volition? Give some example in my life where I was aware of divine power—but working through human intermediaries with their flaws and problems.

The prison ship's warden Julius wrote up an official journal of what happened on board. Since calamity makes strange bedfellows and our voyage certainly fell into such an experience, he and I became acquainted, and he shared his document with me.

# Chapter 26

**To: Caesar**

**Military Log, the Centurion Julius, Ides of November**

**Re: Conducting Imperial Prisoners**

We transferred at the port of Myra in Lycia from the coastal ship bound for Adramyttium, and now are onboard an Alexandrian craft bound for Italy on the high seas. Progress is slow and we find ourselves significantly off-course, pushed under Crete instead of above it. We anchor here, pausing to consider the risks of continuing the voyage. While we delay, the prisoner Paul voiced his opinion that danger lay ahead of us. I am anxious to station ourselves in a more strategic place for favorable winds, so I and the ship officers decided to make a dash for a better harbor only a short distance away. Paul the citizen-prisoner is secure.

> Acts 27:4–11  **4** And putting to sea from there we sailed under the lee of Cyprus, because the winds were against us.  **5** And when we had sailed across the sea which is off Cilicia and Pamphylia, we came to Myra in Lycia.  **6** There the centurion found a ship of Alexandria sailing for Italy, and put us on board.  **7** We sailed slowly for a number of days, and arrived with difficulty off Cnidus, and as the wind did not allow us to go on, we sailed under the lee of Crete off Salmone.  **8** Coasting along it with difficulty, we came to a place called Fair Havens, near which was the city of Lasea.  **9** As much time had been lost, and the voyage was already dangerous because the fast had already gone by, Paul advised them,  **10** saying, "Sirs, I perceive that the voyage will be with injury and much loss, not only of the cargo and the ship, but also of our lives."  **11** But the

centurion paid more attention to the captain and to the owner of the ship than to what Paul said.

## To: Caesar

### Military Log, Julius, vicesimus November

### Re: Conducting Imperial Prisoners

Our day for journeying began in torpor and ended in typhoon. We were so captured by this tempest that all we could do is give way. By our own estimation, we figure we have tooled so far off-course that the shoals of North Africa might loom ahead as our graveyard. Even this danger is drowned out by another threat: the storm wind could easily capsize our craft; and so we begin to jettison our cargo and then all unnecessary ship gear.

With no sky or stars visible, only cloudy shroud and lashing rain, we really had no idea of where we were or even which direction we were heading. This may be my last log entry. Paul the prisoner is safe.

## To: Caesar

### Military Log, Julius, vicesimus primus November

### Re: Conducting Imperial Prisoners

Yesterday we were at our wit's end. The crisis had so levelled status and ranking on board that Paul the prisoner seized an opportunity to speak to everyone. He had advised us before, but we ignored him. This time, however, he riveted us with a report about a nocturnal visitation from his native deity. And he stood before us like a Pythian oracle with a prediction that bucked us all up: none of us would lose our lives. I need not add that desperate men cling to shards of such hope like this. Suffice it to say that from that time on, Paul captures our attention.

> Acts 27:23–26 **23** "For this very night there stood by me an angel of the God to whom I belong and whom I worship, **24** and he said, 'Do not be afraid, Paul; you must stand before Caesar; and lo, God has granted you all those who sail with you.' **25** So take heart, men, for I have faith in God that it will be exactly as I have been told. **26** But we shall have to run on some island."

## To: Caesar

## Military Log, Julius, vicesimus sextus November

## Re: Conducting Imperial Prisoners

After a fortnight of trackless drifting, depth soundings indicate we are fast approaching solid ground. The former fears of crashing into some unseen cliff return. Unknown to me and to the other guards on board, the ship's more seasoned sailors conspire together to abandon ship. Here again Paul is uncannily aware of their plot: he alerts us and warns that if the sailors bolted, the rest of us would be lost. I immediately grasp his point and cut off this option.

Same day, Paul stuns us: He calls for a repast to be hosted by his deity. The whole ritual is reminiscent of a public liturgy put on by temple priests to betoken a god's patronage. Stranger yet, we all join in the revelry! A bizarre sight: 276 souls living for the moment, though their life tottered on the jaws of Hades. Even I madly gorge myself—we had not consumed a bite over the whole time of the storm. And then, as if we had no need of food again, we ceremoniously dumped our remaining supplies into the sea. Our parody meant either there was no limit to the deity's providence—or there was no tomorrow for drowning ship rats. Paul chooses the former view that we would live because of the intervention of his deity. Whatever our sanity, the meal at sea brings us reassurance that our fate is tied up with the prisoner Paul. Paul the prisoner remains secure.

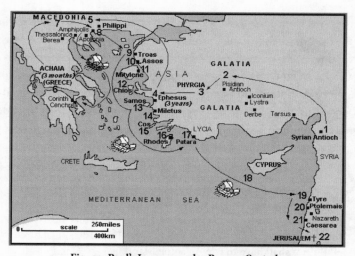

**Fig. 10: Paul's Journey under Roman Custody**

## Chapter 27

### Eucharist?

Let me try to offer my perspective of what you have just heard from Julius's notes. Paul had so risen in stature among the passengers on this boat that we regarded him as a good-luck charm—or even better, the embodiment of Jesus. He is not just on the receiving end of a centurion's hospitality, but advising the centurion about what to do. Even the ship's seasoned sailors and officers eventually bend to his wishes. All the people packed on this barque skimming a sea of oblivion, all 276 souls, see him as their only window of light. So they desperately cling to his every word. Why do they cede such authority to Paul? I don't think they even raised the question.

Inexplicably empowered, Paul takes up Jesus's words that "the Father knows even the number of the hairs on your head! Fear not, little flock," when he says they will not suffer harm and so should show courage. And then all eyes remain fixed as he breaks bread and gives thanks—I use the verb "to eucharistize" when I describe what he did.

Was it the same as the Eucharist service in our communities, Theophilus? At least it shares in our duty to give thanks in all circumstances. For us, though, our blessing went beyond ritualism: the consumption of this food triggered an upward vision for many of us that the current chaotic circumstances actually could unite with some ultimate purpose of God. When we looked at Paul and considered our plight, every soul was cheered and relieved in the face of catastrophe. It was a moment of transfiguration that plucked up our souls from earthbound woes and unified all with a heavenly surge of joy. A more beatific sense of Eucharist could not be conjured up by the most intentional liturgy.

All were filled physically, all were encouraged spiritually! The irony is that this seemingly desperate act was not merely a shaman's shot in the dark to placate supernatural forces, but the means by which the boat was lightened enough to make it seaworthy—simultaneously giving strength to everyone onboard if and when they would have to swim for their lives.

In the glow of this sacramental act, indeed everyone's life would be saved—the angel's word to Paul fulfilled. It was, as it were, divine show for the pleasure of the One seated in the heavens, inviting us all to rejoice.

> Acts 27:31–38 **31** Paul said to the centurion and the soldiers, "Unless these men stay in the ship, you cannot be saved." **32** Then the soldiers cut away the ropes of the boat, and let it go. **33** As day was about to dawn, Paul urged them all to take some food, saying, "Today is the fourteenth day that you have continued in suspense and without food, having taken nothing. **34** Therefore I urge you to take some food; it will give you strength, since not a hair is to perish from the head of any of you." **35** And when he had said this, he took bread, and giving thanks to God in the presence of all he broke it and began to eat. **36** Then they all were encouraged and ate some food themselves. **37** (We were in all two hundred and seventy-six persons in the ship.) **38** And when they had eaten enough, they lightened the ship, throwing out the wheat into the sea.

1. How would we be "life preservers" for those around us in our daily responses to divine plans?

2. How can I be more cognizant of what I might say for the benefit of those around us?

3. Can I encourage our fellow sojourners in life that the Almighty is with us and therefore with them?

4. How about asking God for an angel to come to our assistance when our strength is gone?

## Run Aground

Such delirium, even anchored to some spiritual reality, is temporary. Eventually its buzz wears off, and we return to our normal thought modes. Only the centurion remains in awe of Paul, probably because he had recorded the events for later meditation or because he is in such proximity to Paul for the rest of the journey.

When the ship runs aground and begins to disintegrate, everyone's first thought is to kill the imperial prisoners so that they cannot escape. This is Roman policy. Again Paul springs to action and urges restraint upon the soldiers. Heeding this advice, the centurion saves Paul and thus sets the precedent for the others. And thus the ancient proverb is fulfilled: the presence of the righteous man makes the whole city (or should I say, prison ship?) rejoice.[1]

> Acts 27:42–44 **42** The soldiers' plan was to kill the prisoners, lest any should swim away and escape; **43** but the centurion, wishing to save Paul, kept them from carrying out their purpose. He ordered those who could swim to throw themselves overboard first and make for the land, **44** and the rest on planks or on pieces of the ship. And so it was that all escaped to land.

1. What kind of influence do we/I have with surrounding authorities in public settings?

2. How about with those otherwise casual bystanders: how do they look to us for inspiration and direction?

## Sabbatical

We washed up on shore, one by one, all of us saved. So stunned were we by the ordeal at sea that we wandered about in a stupor. For the ship castaways, the whole fortnight storm and the giddy banquet at sea all now seemed like a dim dream, only groggily remembered. The dreary rain kept falling, and we were freezing. Only Paul seemed to keep his bearing on shore, as if the dream lived on and he knew its outcome.

The natives of that place, though, regarded us as superhumans. After all, they had witnessed the disintegration of the ship, the throng of passengers swimming for their lives, and the miraculous survival of us all. The gods must have particularly favored us as refugees and chosen us as deputies among mortals. So they welcomed us as omens of divine visitation.

For us the storm was a harrowing ordeal; for them it was a windfall, a blessing from the gods. Funny how all of us medicate uncontrollable forces

---

1. Prov 11:10.

with homespun remedies and interpretations! Perhaps not altogether evil, we plod on as children, tossed to and fro by our limited perspectives; and so we often miss the core of what is really going on.

For Paul, Aristarchus, and me, this strange land's reaction was no stranger than any of our travel stops over the years, whether in Asia Minor, Macedonia, or Greece. This land was Malta, an island south of Italy. (This by itself was a miracle that we were still on course!) As the Maltese received us, they studied our every action for signs of divine communication. When they noticed that Paul was stung by a poison snake, they concluded that that the ship brought at least one brute who was cursed, surely a murderer or traitor. When he did not keel over and die, then the popular opinion swung the other way: Paul must be a god over the others. Certainly those who witnessed Paul on board the ship and foggily remembered his actions were inclined toward this latter impression.

The island's residents carried reports of the whole thing to their leader named Publius. And, once again, Paul was the center of attention. Publius's father was sick with fever and diarrhea, and Paul touched him to bring relief. This miracle opened up the whole island to him and to us—all 276 of us as Paul's entourage. We stayed as visiting dignitaries for a whole three months. The Maltese spared nothing in hospitality. The atmosphere was something like a prolonged holiday, as we waited for winter to lift and continue our journey to Rome.

> Acts 28:1–10 [1]After we had escaped, we then learned that the island was called Malta. [2] And the natives showed us unusual kindness, for they kindled a fire and welcomed us all, because it had begun to rain and was cold. [3] Paul had gathered a bundle of sticks and put them on the fire, when a viper came out because of the heat and fastened on his hand. [4] When the natives saw the creature hanging from his hand, they said to one another, "No doubt this man is a murderer. Though he has escaped from the sea, justice has not allowed him to live." [5] He, however, shook off the creature into the fire and suffered no harm. [6] They waited, expecting him to swell up or suddenly fall down dead; but when they had waited a long time and saw no misfortune come to him, they changed their minds and said that he was a god. [7] Now in the neighborhood of that place were lands belonging to the chief man of the island, named Publius, who received us and entertained us hospitably for three days. [8] It happened that the father of Publius lay sick with fever and dysentery; and Paul visited him and prayed, and putting his hands on him healed him. [9] And when this had

taken place, the rest of the people on the island who had diseases also came and were cured. **10** They presented many gifts to us; and when we sailed, they put on board whatever we needed.

1. Do I remember times when I feared I would lose everything in a venture, and wound up losing nothing? Did I experience God showing me "salvation" through this brush with fate? What did I learn from this experience?

2. Give examples of public mood swings for public figures and celebrities, maybe in the realm of politics or sports.

3. How does my public reputation determine how I act or make decisions? How does it determine how I evaluate success or failure?

4. What does God want me to take away from this story about how the public changes its opinions?

# Chapter 28

## Homecoming

We made good progress, once we left Malta. Though we all had regarded Malta as an incredible relief from perils, Paul doggedly reminded us of our goal: Rome and Caesar. The grapevine had passed on the word that Paul was coming, and native believers offered us comfort and welcome as we traveled along the route. Once the Italian landmarks and sites presaged our safe arrival, Paul let his guard down and sobbed with relief: we were near the finish line. The journey was completed, the divine revelation twice given fulfilled. Rome! You can imagine us kissing the ground, Theophilus—but was this the Promised Land, or was it the beginning of a new adventure?

> Acts 28:15 And the brethren there, when they heard of us, came as far as the Forum of Appius and Three Taverns to meet us. On seeing them Paul thanked God and took courage.

1. How has God faithfully brought me home from some big adventure? Give examples.

2. What adventure do I feel I am on now, within which I once again must rely on divine faithfulness?

## Rewind

After a three-year hiatus from the active life, Paul picked up where he left off, testifying to the grace of God. Even in Rome, though, he must bide his time before he would stand in front of Caesar. So in the meantime, he once again takes up the cause among his own people in Rome. Paul had failed so

164

often to win adherents, but never gave up. Thanks to the impression Paul had left with his Roman custodians and travel hosts and companions, he received permission to continue his public activities. Fortunately for his preaching, Judean antagonists in Rome did not have the clout they had in Jerusalem.

> Acts 28:17–20 **17** After three days he called together the local leaders of the Jews; and when they had gathered, he said to them, "Brethren, though I had done nothing against the people or the customs of our fathers, yet I was delivered prisoner from Jerusalem into the hands of the Romans. **18** When they had examined me, they wished to set me at liberty, because there was no reason for the death penalty in my case. **19** But when the Jews objected, I was compelled to appeal to Caesar—though I had no charge to bring against my nation. **20** For this reason therefore I have asked to see you and speak with you, since it is because of the hope of Israel that I am bound with this chain."

1. Have there been times when we frequently failed but felt compelled to keep trying? Describe them.

2. Have there been times when I knew something was going to happen, but could do nothing but simply wait and bide my time? How did it feel?

## True Healing

Have you ever read about the prophet Isaiah? He was commissioned by a seraph from the heavenly throne to go forth on a divine mission, but the recipients of his message subsequently and utterly reject him. After his mountain-top experience with the Almighty, Isaiah spectacularly plunges into utter failure.

The reason for the rejection of Isaiah's message has to do with a near pathological condition of the audience: their heart is sluggish, their ears plugged up with heaviness (wax?), and their eyes are "mystified" (closed?). What is required is "healing," but healing can only come with conversion. And so, Theophilus, who is responsible? By this time in his life, Paul had reckoned with bracing doses of success and (many) failures. He knew that he once rejected the Way—and actually colluded in its persecution—and remarkably had done so with good conscience! Even the best preaching depends to a certain degree on divine grace, an intervention that tears away the scales of unbelief, as it had done for Paul himself. Meanwhile, Paul would wait for this mysterious visitation to unfold in its time. He would fight the good fight, but would leave the rest to the Almighty, blessed be he.

> Acts 28:26–27  **26** 'Go to this people, and say, You shall indeed hear but never understand, and you shall indeed see but never perceive.  **27** For this people's heart has grown dull, and their ears are heavy of hearing, and their eyes they have closed; lest they should perceive with their eyes, and hear with their ears, and understand with their heart, and turn for me to heal them.'

1. Read 1 Pet 2:24 and compare to this passage. How can I pray for my own complete healing?

2. How do I pray in the same way for others?

## Unfinished

Two years pass as Paul continues his mission, staying as long in Rome as he stayed in Ephesus. It has been five years now since Paul made that fateful decision to return to Jerusalem. Where will this all eventually lead? If he turned the city upside down in Ephesus with the news of the Kingdom of God, why not in Rome as well?

Or would it lead to the ultimate testimony in this city, his martyrdom? Initially, he had felt it would be Jerusalem as the ancient prophecies predicted for prophets, but did he exchange this literal expectation with a finale in an allegorized location? If he was martyred in Rome, he knew it would have a huge impact on the momentum and establishment of the church there. If he stayed longer and did not die there, well . . . my story does not say. And I do not say here, Theophilus, because not then nor now is it over.

But all around there is an unmistakable impression that Paul has done nothing deserving death. Perhaps his lifelong dream of going to Spain would be fulfilled, if only he could be released from his impending verdict. Which ending does my retelling seem to imply? Even more, Theophilus, what does it imply for you and your own life's testimony?

> Acts 28:30–31  **30** And he lived there two whole years at his own expense, and welcomed all who came to him,  **31** preaching the kingdom of God and teaching about the Lord Jesus Christ quite openly and unhindered.

1. How would I answer these last questions above, now that I have finished the narrative?

2. How would I want my life to end if I were Paul?

3. What is my impression of the timetable surrounding Paul? How about the timetable surrounding my life and its outcome?

## Postscript

This is where I stop, but where my performance stops and your life continues is up to you. I have striven to tell a history here as if it were reenacted before your eyes. In my clumsy and half-cultured ways, I have tried to tell a good story, to engage you, and then to withdraw. You may charge me, reader, with taking poetic license, but in reality every historian takes such liberties. The secret for the historian is to revive the past in a way that accounts for the facts and that engages the audience's present. In this unfinished tale, I tell a history by neither repeating the past nor by preaching something imaginary. Rather I perform.

# Name/Subject Index

169

# Scripture Index